EQUIVALENTS

Butter or margarine.........1 stick (¼ lb.) = ½ cup

Buttermilk...1 cup = 1-2 tablespoons vinegar with sweet milk to fill cup (let stand 5 minutes)

Chocolate........1 square = 3 tablespoons cocoa plus 1 tablespoon butter

Cream....1 cup whipping cream = 2 cups or more after whipping

Eggs......................2 large eggs = 3 small eggs

Macaroni...................1 cup = 2¼ cups cooked

Rice.......................1 cup = 4 cups cooked

Shortening....................1 pound = 2½ cups

Sugar, brown..1 pound = 2¼-2½ cups (firmly packed)
confectioners'........1 pound = 4-4½ cups (sifted)
granulated..................1 pound = 2¼ cups

Thickening.....1 tablespoon quick cooking tapioca = 1 tablespoon cornstarch or 1½ tablespoons flour

CONTENTS

		Page
	Aluminum Is Friendly To Foods	3
	Wear-Ever Preferred	6
	All-New Wear-Ever, The Ultimate	7
NEW	Aluminum Cooks Best	8
METHOD	How To Cook New Method	9
COOKING	If You Have A Gas Range	10
	Burner With a Brain	11-13
	If You Have An Electric Range	14, 15
	How To Clean New Method Utensils	16
APPETIZERS,	Utensil Combinations For Appetizers, Soups, Beverages	18
SOUPS, BEVERAGES	Appetizer, Soup and Beverage Recipes	19-24
	Utensil Combinations For Vegetables	26
	Directions For Cooking Fresh Vegetables	27
	Directions For Cooking Quick Frozen Vegetables	28
VEGETABLES	Vegetable Recipes	29-34
	Vegetable Sauces	35
	Vegetable Buying Guide	36
	Utensil Combinations For Fruits	38
	Directions For Cooking Fruits, Berries	39
FRUITS	Fruit Recipes	39-42
	Fruit Buying Guide	42
	Utensil Combinations For Dried Foods, Puddings	44, 45
	Directions For Cooking Dried Foods	46-48
DRIED FOODS,	Dried Foods Recipes	47-49
AND PUDDINGS	Directions For Cooking Puddings	50
	Pudding Recipes	50-52
	Pudding Sauces	52
	Utensil Combinations For Meats, Fowl, Fish	54-56
	Directions For Top of Range Roasting	57-59
	Directions For Pan Broiling	57, 58
	Directions For Use of Large Rectangular Roaster	58
MEATS, FOWL	Meat, Fowl and Fish Recipes	59-71
AND FISH	Egg, Cheese Recipes	72
	Stuffing Recipes	73, 74
	Meat, Poultry, Fish Sauces	74, 75
	Meat, Poultry, Fish Buying Guide	76
	Utensil Combinations For Top of Range Baking	78, 79
	Directions For Top of Range Baking	80, 81
TOP OF RANGE	Cake Recipes and Cake Icings	81-87
BAKING	Pie and Cookie Recipes	88-91
	Quick Breads and Yeast Breads	91-95
	Griddle Cakes, French Toast	96
GUARANTEE	Wear-Ever New Method Guarantee	97

WEAR-EVER NEW METHOD COOK BOOK
by Margaret Mitchell
Twenty-first Edition Copyright 1960
Wear-Ever Aluminum, Inc. New Kensington, Pa.
Designed and Illustrated by Frank Marcello
Litho by Haynes Lithograph Co., Rockville, Md.

Almost all the foods we eat contain Aluminum — Nature put it there

ALUMINUM
is friendly to foods

Aluminum, so geologists tell us, is the most abundant of all the metallic elements found in the earth's crust. In fact, approximately 8% of the surface layer of the earth is aluminum, while only about 5% is iron. Thus, it is easy to understand why aluminum plays such an important part in the lives of the human race.

Yes, aluminum is friendly to food. Scientists tell us that it forms a part of practically all food we eat, even drinking water. It is found, in minute quantities, in such common foods as potatoes, oranges, apples, meats and milk, to name only a few.

And so, you see, your daily diet includes a certain amount of aluminum along with the other essential mineral elements such as iron, calcium, magnesium and phosphorus.

Aluminum, then, is the most nearly ideal among all the materials which are practical for the manufacture of cooking utensils. Like china or glass it does not affect food color, flavor or wholesomeness.

The WEAR-EVER Kitchens

The Wear-Ever Kitchens at New Kensington are considered among the finest and most authoritative in the country.

In the Wear-Ever Kitchens, Margaret Mitchell and her assistants put experimental models of new utensils through exacting tests before manufacturing for sale. Further checks on the acceptability of WEAR-EVER Utensils are provided by established homemakers, and Home Economists of America's leading woman's magazines.

Dear Friend:

Congratulations! You are now the proud owner of the most beautiful and efficient utensils ever made. They are yours to use and enjoy for many years to come.

Wear-Ever means finest quality and the New Method of Cooking assures you of maximum nutrition in the foods you prepare.

Because the cover on each pan is precision fitted so that every drop of precious moisture is kept in the pan, vegetables and fruits can be cooked without added water. The even heating of aluminum makes it possible to prepare meats without the use of fat. Dried foods are easily restored to a plump and tender state, while cakes, moist and feather light, can be baked on top of the range.

All this could be called Kitchen Magic. But it is simple magic when you follow the cooking instructions and the recipes found in each food section of this exclusive New Method Cookbook.

We suggest you follow them exactly. It may take a little experimenting on your part to determine just the right heat to use on your particular range, but the results are worth this effort.

When used as directed, the Wear-Ever New Method of Cooking will help you prepare daily meals that are nutritious, and enable you and your family to enjoy good eating for many years to come.

Sincerely,

Margaret Mitchell
DIRECTOR OF HOME ECONOMICS
WEAR-EVER ALUMINUM, INC.

WEAR-EVER
preferred by hospitals, hotels and restaurants

What higher recommendation could there be!

Wear-Ever Aluminum Utensils are used daily in . . .

Hundreds of Hospitals . . .

Other Hospitals:

Massachusetts General Hospital, Boston
Johns Hopkins Hospital, Baltimore
Allegheny General Hospital, Pittsburgh
Battle Creek Sanitarium, Battle Creek, Mich.
Jefferson Memorial Hospital, Birmingham
U. S. Marine Hospital, San Francisco
Los Angeles County General Hospital
Cook County Hospital, Chicago
Kansas City Medical Center
St. John's Hospital, St. Louis
University Hospital, Columbus, Ohio
Texas Children's Hospital, Dallas

Presbyterian Medical Center, Columbia University, one of world's largest hospitals, is equipped with Wear-Ever Aluminum.

Thousands of Hotels and Restaurants . . .

Other Hotels:

Palmer House, Chicago
Fontainebleau Hotel, Miami Beach
Carlton House, Pittsburgh
Desi-Lu Western Hills Lodge, Calif.

Famous Restaurants:

Antoine's, New Orleans
Schrafft Restaurants
Stouffer Restaurants
Howard Johnson Restaurants

Hotel New Yorker, New York City, a heavy user of Wear-Ever hotel equipment.

and, of course, in millions of American homes!

ALL NEW
WEAR-EVER
the ULTIMATE *in* STYLING
BEAUTY
CONVENIENCE
DURABILITY
EFFICIENCY

outstanding ALL NEW *design features*

1 Full-Sweep Cover—Gives distinctive styling and added cooking space . . . fits perfectly.

2 Alumilite Finish—Stain-resistant finish on covers . . . in choice of exciting colors for pleasing contrast and striking appearance.

3 Bakelite Knob—Smartly styled—cool, large enough to give a firm grip.

4 Handle—Exclusive, sleek-looking, easy-grip bakelite handle with stainless steel shaft to keep it cool.

5 Hang-up Loop—Unique, convenient hang-up loop. Wear-Ever fits any kitchen decor and adds a quiet touch of beauty and quality.

6 Thick Aluminum Sides and Bottom—Spread heat evenly and quickly through pan, making New Method cooking possible.

7 Round Easy-to-Clean Corners—Cleaning inside can be done in a jiffy.

7

ALUMINUM COOKS BEST

SUPERIOR HEAT CONDUCTIVITY...

...MAKES WEAR-EVER NEW METHOD COOKING POSSIBLE:

No additional water is needed with New Method Aluminum Utensils. The entire pan cooks the food . . . from the bottom up, from the sides in, and from the top down. This avoids hot-spot scorching . . . making it possible for foods to cook in their own natural juices.

Aluminum spreads heat 3 to 8 times faster

COMPARE HEAT CONDUCTIVITY OF METALS MOST OFTEN USED IN COOKING UTENSILS

Figures represent C.G.S. units, the scientific scale by which heat conductivity of metals and alloys is measured and compared.

.46 aluminum

.15 copper-coated steel

.11 cast iron

.06 stainless steel

How to cook by

NEW METHOD

It is easy to prepare food by the Wear-Ever New Method of Cooking if you follow a few simple instructions. Here are the fundamental rules that assure success:

know the pan to use

The proper utensils and combinations to use for cooking all types of food are shown at the beginning of each food division in this exclusive New Method Cookbook. For your convenience in selecting the pan specified in a recipe, each utensil has its number stamped on the bottom.

a. When cooking fruits and vegetables select a pan the food will most nearly fill. Never attempt to cook a small quantity in a large pan.

b. Always use cover designed to fit pan.

c. Do not remove cover except to test for doneness near end of cooking time.

know the heat to use

See complete directions and explanation of heat terms for your particular range on the following pages. In general:

When cooking fruits and vegetables—
  start on medium heat until cover is hot to touch or wisps of steam escape—about 5 minutes. Reduce heat to low for remainder of cooking time.

When cooking meats—
  preheat broiler or roaster pan on high heat until a piece of white paper starts to turn brown; reduce heat to medium. Use medium heat to brown all meats. For longer cooking reduce heat to low.

When cooking dried foods—
  bring water in bottom pan to boil on high heat; reduce heat to low.

When baking on top of the range over direct heat—
  start on medium heat; reduce heat to low after 5 minutes unless recipe instructions read otherwise.

When using the large rectangular roaster as an "oven"—
  follow the general directions on page 80 as well as those given in the recipes.

It's easy when you learn

The Wear-Ever New Method Equipment can be used on any range. The important thing is to learn first the meaning of our terms for heat regulation. Study directions for your particular range before you start cooking and remember the rule: Save heat and you will save money

IF YOU HAVE A GAS RANGE

1. USE HIGH HEAT—
flame just touching bottom of utensil . . .

To preheat all utensils for browning meats.
To preheat pan for baking griddle cakes.
To preheat No. 825 rectangular roaster when used as an "oven." See baking directions.
To boil water over which to steam dried foods.
Adjust height of flame under pan until it just touches the bottom.
<u>Never</u> turn flame so high that it flares up around sides of pan.

2. USE MEDIUM HEAT—
flame half as high as High . . .

To brown roasts, steaks, chops.
To pan broil steaks, chops.
To bake griddle cakes.
To start fresh fruits, vegetables until cover becomes hot to touch.
To start direct top of range baking. See baking directions.

3. USE LOW OR SIMMER HEAT—
flame barely visible . . .

To cook less tender cuts of meat after browning.
To cook roasts after browning.
To cook fresh fruits, vegetables after cover becomes hot to touch.
To steam dried foods over water after water boils.
To do direct top of range baking after utensil has been heated.

If you have a Gas range equipped with
A "BURNER WITH A BRAIN"

Place the utensil on the thermostatic or controlled heat top burner so that the sensing element (the "eye" is in the center of the burner) comes in contact with the bottom of the utensil. Turn the control to the desired temperature. The sensing element measures the heat in the utensil and will automatically adjust the flame to maintain the set temperature.

The thermostatic top burner may also be equipped with an additional automatic control called "Flame Set" or "Flame Selector." Because Wear-Ever aluminum utensils conduct the heat so evenly, this special control for adjusting the size of the flame is unnecessary and should be disregarded. Follow the simple instructions:

1. Turn dial to "HI" to light burner.
2. Then turn dial to proper temperature for cooking.

When using the "Burner with a Brain" follow the recipes in the book for pre-preparation instruction and the following charts for temperature and time.

APPETIZERS, SOUPS, BEVERAGES—RECIPES PAGES 19-24

	DIAL SETTING	TIME (MINUTES)
Pan-Broiled Grapefruit Half	200°	10-15
Anchovy Squares	325°	5
Consommé Madrilene	200°	1 hour
Tomato Bouillon		
To brown meat	325°	
Simmer ingredients	200°	3 hours
Spinach and Onion Soup		
To cook bacon	275°	5-8
To cook cream sauce	200°	8-10
Cream Soups—cook white sauce	200°	8-10
Oyster Bisque	200°	15-20
Indian Corn Soup	200°	15-20
Dried Navy Bean Soup		
To cook beans	212°	1½ hours
Simmer ingredients	200°	20
Consommé Julienne		
Bring to boil	220°	
Simmer ingredients	200°	15-20
Borsch	200°	15-20
Drip Coffee—to boil water	240°	
Percolator Coffee	240°	7-10
Holding temperature for coffee	190°	
Cocoa	200°	20

VEGETABLES—RECIPES PAGES 29-34

FRESH VEGETABLES	DIAL SETTING	TIME (MINUTES)
Asparagus	200°	25-30
Artichokes	200°	40-45
Beans, Green or Yellow	200°	25-30
Beans, Lima	200°	25-30
Beets, sliced	200°	25-30
whole	200°	35-40
Harvard Sauce	200°	5
Beet Greens	190°	18-20
Broccoli	200°	20-25
Brussels Sprouts	200°	25-30
Cabbage, wedges	200°	20
shredded	200°	15
Carrots, sliced or small whole	200°	30-35
Cauliflower, flowerets	200°	15-20
whole	200°	30-35

VEGETABLES—RECIPES PAGES 29-34 (Continued)

FRESH VEGETABLES	DIAL SETTING	TIME (MINUTES)
Celery, diced	200°	25-30
Corn on the Cob	225°	30-35
Eggplant	375°	8-10
Kale	190°	30-35
Kohlrabi, sliced	200°	25
quartered	200°	35
Creamed Mushrooms	200°	8-10
Mushrooms, (pan ⅔ full)		
sliced	175°	30
whole	175°	35
Onions	200°	30-35
Parsnips	200°	35-40
Peas (pan ⅔ full)	200°	20-25
Baked Potatoes	375°	60
Candied Sweet Potatoes	200°	60
to thicken syrup	225°	10
Georgian Sweet Potatoes	375°	45-50
to heat after ricing	200°	10-15
Pumpkin	200°	40-45
Rutabaga, pared, diced	200°	35-40
Spinach	200°	10-12
and Bacon (fry bacon)	275°	5-10
Squash, Summer	200°	15-20
Squash, Winter	200°	30-35
Swiss Chard	200°	12-15
Tomatoes	200°	15-20
Stuffed Tomatoes	200°	20
Turnips	200°	40-45
Hot Potato Salad		
Potatoes	375°	60
Bacon	275°	5-8
Reheat	200°	10-15

FROZEN VEGETABLES—PAGE 28

Large size vegetables such as: asparagus, broccoli, Brussels sprouts, cauliflower, spinach	200°	15 minutes; stir; 5-10 minutes longer
Small size vegetables such as: corn, peas, mixed vegetables	200°	10 minutes; stir; 10 minutes; stir; 12-15

SAUCES—USED WITH VEGETABLES—PAGE 35

Sauces Used With Vegetables	200°	8-10

FRUITS—RECIPES PAGES 39-42

FRUITS	DIAL SETTING	TIME (MINUTES)
Apple Sauce	200°	30-35
Baked Apples	200°	55-60
Stuffed Apples	200°	55-60
Grilled Apple Rings	250°	10-15
Cinnamon Apples	225°	15-20
Glazed Bananas	250°	10-15
Cranberry Jelly	200°	40
Cranberry Sauce	200°	20-25
Glazed Cranberries	225°	10-15
Pears	200°	20-25
Spiced Peaches	200°	25
Minted Peaches	250°	5-8
Spiced Apricot Goblins	200°	10-15
Cinnamon Pineapple Rings	250°	5-8
Apricot Sauce	212°	30
Paradise Sauce	200°	20
Fresh Fruit Sauce	200°	10-15
Rhubarb Sauce	200°	10-15
Strawberry-Rhubarb Sauce	200°	15

MEATS, FOWL, FISH, EGGS, CHEESE—RECIPES PAGES 59-75

MEATS, FOWL, FISH, EGGS, CHEESE	DIAL SETTING	TIME (MINUTES)
Roasts—brown at	325°	See recipe
reduce to	225°	See recipe
Meat Loaves	200°	See recipe
Pan Broiling	325°	See recipe
Bacon, frying	275°	5-8 min.
Braising—brown at	325°	See recipe
reduce to	225°	See recipe
Poaching Fish	200°	See recipe
Steaming Fish	212°	See recipe
Sauces and Gravies	200°	8-10
Eggs—Cheese	200°	See recipe

DRIED FOODS AND PUDDINGS—RECIPES PAGES 47-52

DRIED FOOD	DIAL SETTING	TIME (MINUTES)
Cereals	212°	see page 46
Vegetables	212°	1-2 hours
Fruits	212°	30-45
Macaroni, Spaghetti, Noodles	212°	30 min.; stir; 10 minutes
Tamale Rice with Frankfurters		
sauté onions	275°	5-10
simmer ingredients	200°	15
steam	212°	35-40
Tallarene		
sauté onions, meat	275°	10-15
simmer ingredients	200°	10
steam	212°	40-45
American spaghetti		
brown ham	275°	10
simmer ingredients	200°	10
Baked Macaroni, Ham & Cheese		
cream sauce	200°	8-10
steam	212°	15-20
Puddings, steamed	212°	see recipes
Baked custard	275°	20
Chocolate sauce	200°	6-8

TOP OF RANGE BAKING—RECIPES PAGES 81-95

CAKE	DIAL SETTING	TIME (MINUTES)
Milk Chocolate	275°	60
Sour Cream Devil's Food Cake	275°	70
Dark Devil's Food Cake	275°	45-50
Coconut Silver Cake	275°	40-45
Butter Cream Cake	275°	35-40
Applesauce Cake	275°	35-40
Pineapple Upside Down Cake	275°	45
Sour Milk Gingerbread	275°	50
Prize Spice Cake	275°	45
Mincemeat Fruit Cake	260°	1 hr. 45 min.
Banana Nut Cake	260°	40
Cream Sponge Cake	300°	35-40
Orange Chiffon Cake	300°	60
Small Orange Chiffon Cake	275°	35-40
Angel Food Cake	300°	45

ICINGS	DIAL SETTING	TIME (MINUTES)
Boiled Icing	300°	12
Sea Foam Topping	300°	6-7
Fudge Icing	275°	12-15
Chocolate Confectioners' Frosting	200°	5

QUICK BREADS	DIAL SETTING	TIME (MINUTES)
Baking Powder Biscuits	300°	10; turn; 10 min.
French Coffee Cake	200°	1 hr. 15 min.
Cinnamon Pecan Rolls	275°	20-25
Coffee Cake—batter	275°	15
topping	275°	35
Cornbread	200°	30
Old Fashioned Rich Doughnuts	375°	3-4

13

General information

NEW METHOD COOKERY ON ELECTRIC RANGE

1. Acquaint yourself with your electric range so you know approximately what heat is obtainable when the switches are set at different speeds. Once you have determined the best heat to use for a cooking operation, make a note of it for future reference.

2. Remember the electric range unit heats quickly and maintains a high degree of heat. Therefore, follow timing for various switch positions in the recipe and reduce heat immediately. If the unit is too hot at the switch position specified, turn switch lower or to "off" for several minutes, then back to the lowest heat.

3. Because Wear-Ever utensils are made of heavy cold rolled sheet aluminum and conduct heat rapidly and distribute it evenly, the lowest heat available on the range is all that is necessary for most New Method Cooking procedures. If part of the unit is exposed around the pan it does not impair the cooking efficiency. In general, use the unit your pan most nearly fits.

4. Most modern electric ranges are provided with five speed units. The "simmer" on this unit is ideal for New Method Vegetable Cookery. While it is convenient to have such a heat on your range, it is by no means essential to successful New Method Cooking.

5. If your electric range top is of porcelain enamel, it may craze or crack if subjected to too quick a change in temperature or too intense a heat. Therefore, do not place a hot pan on the cold surface. Never use a pan on high heat if it extends over the enamel unless the porcelain is protected by a sheet of asbestos or a similar insulating material.

If you have

AN ELECTRIC RANGE

USE HIGH HEAT
—"Medium-High" Switch Position.

To preheat all utensils for browning meats.
To preheat pan for baking griddle cakes.
To boil water over which to steam dried foods.
Place pan on cold unit, heating gradually with unit. <u>Do not</u> place cold pan on hot unit.

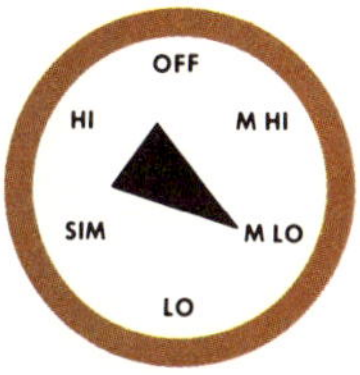

USE MEDIUM HEAT
—"Medium" or "Medium-Low" Switch Position.

To brown roasts, steaks, chops.
To pan broil steaks, chops.
To bake griddle cakes.
To start fresh fruits, vegetables until cover becomes hot to touch.
To start direct top of range baking. See baking directions.

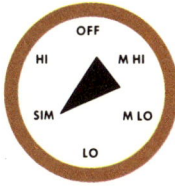

USE LOW HEAT
—"Low" Switch Position.

To cook less tender cuts of meat after browning.
To cook roasts after browning.
To cook fresh fruits, vegetables after cover becomes hot to touch.
To steam dried foods over water after water boils.
To do direct top of range baking after utensil has been heated.

USE SIMMER HEAT
—"Simmer" Switch Position.

To cook fruits, vegetables in No. 771 and 771½ pans after cover becomes hot to touch.

15

How to clean

NEW METHOD UTENSILS

Wear-Ever New Method utensils can be kept clean and bright with a minimum of effort—if you will devote a few minutes each day to their care.

Points on proper care of utensils:

1. After each use, wash utensil in hot sudsy water; rub inside briskly with Wear-Ever cleanser pad; rinse well with clear hot water; dry thoroughly.

2. Because some soaps and detergents contain strong alkalies such as caustic soda, sal soda and potash, use only a mild soap or detergent. Do not allow utensils to soak in dishwater as this may cause them to discolor. Since some detergents combined with local waters can mar the finish, washing utensils in an automatic dishwasher is not recommended.

3. To remove food which may have accidentally burned onto inside of utensil, partially fill pan with boiling water; let stand a few minutes; scrape off burned food with a wooden clothespin or small wooden stick.

4. To remove harmless discoloration caused by minerals present in foods and some waters, boil a solution of two tablespoons cream of tartar per quart water in the pan 10-15 minutes.

5. To polish outside of utensil use any good silver polish.

6. The Alumilite finish on covers can be kept clean and beautiful by washing in hot sudsy water. Do not use steel wool or other abrasives on this finish.

7. To straighten warping or bulges caused by too much heat, place several thicknesses of magazines over bulge and hammer back into shape.

8. If handles or knobs become loose or break, new parts for repairing utensils can be secured through your distributor, or by writing the company.

9. Do not become alarmed if after using your utensils small marks or pits appear. They will affect neither the quality of the food nor reduce the life or usefulness of the utensil.

appetizers, soups and beverages

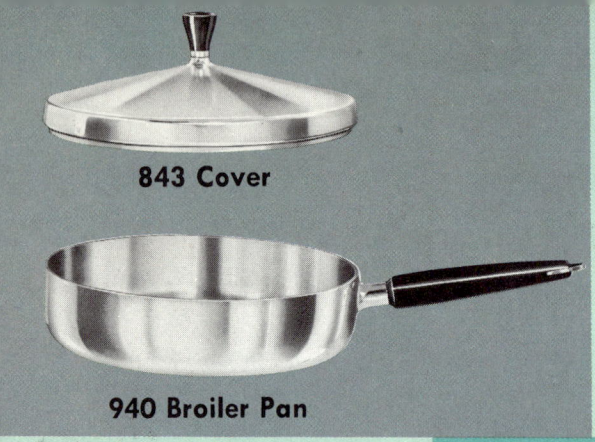
843 Cover

940 Broiler Pan

772 773 774½ Pans and Covers

845 Cover

918 Utility Pan

843 Cover

844 Pan

968 Coffee Maker Combination

WEAR-EVER NEW METHOD UTENSILS FOR...

appetizers, soups, beverages

appetizers, soups, beverages

AVOCADO FREEZE

    4 cups tomato juice
    1 package lemon gelatin
    1/4 teaspoon ground cloves
    1/4 teaspoon paprika
    1/8 teaspoon black pepper
    1 1/4 teaspoons salt
    1 tablespoon onion juice
    Red coloring

1. Heat 1 cup tomato juice; add gelatin; stir until dissolved.
2. Add remaining ingredients; mix well; freeze; stir several times during freezing to distribute seasonings.
3. Freeze to firm but not hard consistency.
4. Serve in unpeeled ripe avocado halves. Garnish with water cress.
5. Ten servings.

HALF GRAPEFRUIT WITH ORANGE JUICE

    3 grapefruit
    3/4 cup orange juice

1. Wash grapefruit; chill thoroughly.
2. Cut grapefruit in half crosswise; remove seeds; separate segments of grapefruit from membrane.
3. Pour orange juice over grapefruit; chill.
4. Sprinkle with confectioner's sugar just before serving.

PINEAPPLE SHRUB

1. Chill pineapple juice until very cold.
2. Pour 1/3 cup juice into each chilled cocktail glass; add 1 tablespoon pineapple sherbet. Serve at once.

MELON BALLS IN GINGER ALE

    Use Honey Dew, Cantaloupe, Watermelon
    2 ripe melons
    1 pint ginger ale

1. Cut melons into halves; scrape out seeds.
2. Using a potato ball cutter, cut out balls.
3. Place 6-8 assorted balls in each sherbet glass; chill.
4. At serving time, cover with chilled ginger ale.
5. Six servings.

CHRISTMAS FRUIT CUP

    4 large grapefruit
    6 large navel oranges
    1 large avocado
    1 pomegranate
    Fresh mint

1. Peel grapefruit, oranges; separate into sections.
2. Pare avocado; remove stone; slice thin.
3. Arrange fruit in glasses.
4. Remove hard outer covering from pomegranate; remove seeds from sacs. Use with mint for garnish.
5. Eight servings.

PAN-BROILED GRAPEFRUIT HALF

    4 grapefruit
    4 tablespoons butter
    ½ cup brown sugar
    8 maraschino cherries

1. Cut grapefruit into halves crosswise.
2. With sharp knife cut around each fruit section, separating fruit from membrane.
3. Melt butter in No. 940 pan over very low heat; sprinkle bottom of pan with brown sugar.
4. Place grapefruit in pan, cut side down over brown sugar.
5. Heat slowly to melt sugar and warm fruit—about 15 minutes.
6. Place cherry in center of each half; pour syrup over fruit just before serving.
7. Thin coating of currant jelly or honey can be used to vary the flavor.

GRAPEFRUIT BASKETS WITH DICED FRUIT

    6 grapefruit
    2 bananas
    ½ pound Tokay grapes
    1 pineapple
    1 bunch mint

1. Across the stem end of four grapefruit cut two parallel lines about ½ inch apart coming almost halfway down the grapefruit.
2. With a small, sharp knife cut into grapefruit along the lines. (This makes the handle of the basket.)
3. Then from each side cut at right angles to meet end of cuts already made.
4. Lift out the two sections cut free—a basket with handle.
5. Cut out all pulp; make fluted edge around basket with knife or scissors.
6. Fill basket with diced banana, seeded cut grapes, grapefruit sections, diced fresh pineapple.
7. Garnish with sprig of mint.

FROSTED CRANBERRY COCKTAIL

    ½ cup cranberry sauce
    ½ teaspoon grated lemon rind
    1 teaspoon lemon juice
    5 tablespoons crushed pineapple with juice or
    3 tablespoons orange juice
    1 egg white, stiffly beaten
    1 pint ginger ale

1. Break up cranberry sauce with fork.
2. Combine cranberry sauce, lemon rind, lemon juice, crushed pineapple with juice; mix well.
3. Pour into tray in freezing compartment of refrigerator. Set cold control at "coldest" position.
4. Freeze until partially frozen.
5. Beat egg whites until stiff but not dry.
6. When cranberry mixture is partially frozen, beat until smooth with electric mixer or rotary egg beater.
7. Fold in stiffly beaten egg whites. Return to tray in freezing compartment. Be sure cold control is at "coldest." When sherbet is completely frozen, return cold control to "normal."
8. Place large spoonful sherbet in bottom of cocktail glass. Fill glass with ginger ale; stir. Note: This bubbles so fill glass slowly.
9. Let stand 1-2 minutes; serve.
10. Six servings.

PINE NECTAR

    1½ cups canned tomato juice
    1½ cups canned unsweetened pineapple juice

1. Combine juices; blend thoroughly.
2. Pour into tray in freezing compartment of refrigerator. Freeze to a mush.
3. Pour into chilled cocktail glasses, allowing about ½ cup per serving. Serve at once.
4. Six servings.

STUFFED CELERY HEARTS

    3 celery hearts
    6 tablespoons Roquefort cheese
    3 tablespoons cream cheese
    Paprika

1. Split celery hearts lengthwise.
2. Blend Roquefort, cream cheese together until smooth.
3. Spread cheese mixture on celery using a fork; sprinkle with paprika.
4. Place on relish tray.
5. Six servings.

SEAFOOD COCKTAIL

    1½ cups cooked, shredded crab meat (approximately 6 ounces)
    1½ cups cooked, shredded whitefish (approximately ½ pound)
    Lettuce hearts
    1 lemon
    ¾ cup Seafood Cocktail Sauce

1. Combine crab meat with whitefish; mix thoroughly; chill.
2. Make a bed of 2-3 lettuce hearts in bottom of cocktail glass.
3. Pile about ½ cup mixed seafood on lettuce.
4. Serve with a lemon wedge, 2 tablespoons cocktail sauce.
5. Six servings.

PINEAPPLE CRAB MEAT COCKTAIL

    Lettuce
    1 6-ounce can crab meat
    ¾ cup canned pineapple, cut into cubes
    ⅓ cup grapefruit sections
    ½ cup mayonnaise
    Dash paprika

1. Line 6 sherbet glasses with lettuce.
2. Flake, remove stiff tendons from crab meat; drain cubed pineapple, grapefruit sections; lightly combine ingredients with mayonnaise.
3. Put into glasses; sprinkle with paprika.
4. Six servings.

ANCHOVY SQUARES

    6 slices white sandwich bread
    8 tablespoons soft butter
    6 tablespoons anchovy paste

1. Cut crust from bread; cut each slice into 4 squares.
2. Place No. 940 pan over medium heat for 3 minutes; reduce heat to low.
3. Spread both sides of bread squares with soft butter; put into hot pan; brown lightly on both sides.
4. Remove to plate; spread with anchovy paste.
5. Yield: 6 servings of 4 squares each.

CONSOMMÉ MADRILENE WITH AVOCADO SLICES

    4 cups chicken stock
    4 cups beef bouillon
    4 cups canned tomatoes
    1 medium onion, sliced
    ½ cup diced carrots
    2 whole cloves
    1 stalk celery
    3 peppercorns
    2 teaspoons salt
    1 teaspoon sugar
    1 avocado, sliced

1. Combine all ingredients except avocado in No. 844 pan; cover.
2. Place over medium heat until steam escapes from under cover.
3. Reduce heat to low; cook 1 hour.
4. Strain; clarify.
5. Serve garnished with sliced avocado.

TO CLARIFY CONSOMMÉ

1. Combine one egg white and crushed shell with 2 tablespoons cold water.
2. Add to consommé; heat slowly to boiling point, stirring constantly.
3. Remove from heat; add ¼ cup cold water; let settle.
4. Strain through 3 thicknesses of cheesecloth. Discard settlings in bottom of pan.
5. Twelve servings.

TOMATO BOUILLON

BASIC BEEF BOUILLON
- 4 pounds beef
- 2½ quarts water
- 1 diced carrot
- 2 medium onions, sliced
- 4 stalks celery, diced
- 2 bay leaves
- 4 cloves
- 10 peppercorns
- 4 sprigs parsley
- ¼ teaspoon thyme
- ¼ teaspoon marjoram
- 3 teaspoons salt

TOMATO BOUILLON
- 5 cups basic beef bouillon
- 2 cups canned tomatoes
- 1 tablespoon minced onion
- 6 whole cloves
- ½ teaspoon celery seed
- 1 small avocado

Directions for Basic Beef Bouillon:
1. Cut meat into cubes; heat No. 844 pan over <u>high</u> heat until a piece of white paper placed in bottom turns brown.
2. Reduce heat to <u>medium</u>; add meat; brown well on all sides.
3. Add remaining ingredients; cover; reduce heat to <u>low</u>; simmer 3 hours.
4. Strain through cheese cloth.

Directions for Tomato Bouillon:
1. Combine beef bouillon with tomatoes, onion, cloves, celery seed; simmer uncovered 20 minutes. Strain in cone of food press; serve at once.
2. Garnish with avocado slices.
3. Eight servings.

SPINACH AND ONION SOUP
- 1 slice bacon
- 1 cup minced onion
- 2 tablespoons flour
- 4 cups milk
- 4 cups spinach pureé
- Salt

1. Cut bacon into small pieces; cook in No. 940 pan until crisp.
2. Add onion; cook until soft, yellow.
3. Add flour; blend well.
4. Transfer to large vegetable pan.
5. Slowly add milk, spinach puree; cook to desired thickness.
6. Season; serve.
7. Six servings.

CREAM SOUPS

General Directions for Standard Cream Soup
- 2 tablespoons fat
- 2 tablespoons flour
- Salt, pepper
- 4 cups milk or part milk and part stock
- 2 cups vegetable pulp or pureé

1. Melt fat; add flour, seasonings.
2. Stir until well blended; add milk gradually while stirring.
3. Bring to boiling point; boil 2 minutes. *This is a White Sauce foundation.*
4. Cook vegetables according to directions; put through food press. *This is a pureé.*
5. Combine vegetables with White Sauce.
6. Season; beat with egg beater; serve. A tiny portion of whipped cream may be used as a garnish.
7. Six servings.
8. Tomatoes, celery, spinach, corn, asparagus, peas may be used.

CREAM OF TOMATO SOUP
- 2 cups tomatoes
- Salt, pepper
- 2 tablespoons butter
- 2 tablespoons flour
- 4 cups milk or half stock, half milk
- ¼ teaspoon soda

1. Cook tomatoes according to directions; put through food press; season.
2. Make white sauce of butter, flour, liquid.
3. Just before serving, add soda to tomatoes; gradually add to white sauce, stirring constantly.
4. Serve at once.
5. Six servings.

OYSTER BISQUE

    3 cups milk, scalded
    ½ tablespoon quick cooking tapioca
    ½ teaspoon salt
    Dash of cayenne pepper
    Dash paprika
    ⅛ cup finely chopped onion
    1 cup raw drained oysters, finely cut
    2 tablespoons butter
    1 tablespoon finely chopped parsley

1. Scald milk in No. 772 pan.
2. Blend tapioca, salt, pepper, paprika, onion. Add milk; cook over low heat 5 minutes; stir frequently.
3. Add oysters, butter; reheat.
4. Allow ½ cup per serving. Sprinkle each serving with parsley. Serve hot.
5. Eight servings.

INDIAN CORN SOUP

    1 cup canned cream style corn
    1 cup canned corn kernels
    1 tablespoon grated onion
    ¼ cup butter
    2 hard cooked egg yolks
    1½ teaspoons flour
    2 teaspoons salt
    ⅛ teaspoon pepper
    1 teaspoon minced parsley
    1 pint milk

1. Combine corn, grated onion.
2. Cream butter; add cooked egg yolks, flour, salt, pepper; mix well.
3. Add to corn mixture; add minced parsley, milk. Heat thoroughly.
4. Four servings.

DRIED NAVY BEAN SOUP

    1 cup dry navy beans
    2 cups cold water
    ½ pound salt pork
    2 cups water
    Pepper and salt

1. Soak beans overnight in 2 cups of water.
2. Arrange No. 844 pan with No. 807 ring and No. 802 pan. Place beans in water in which they were soaked in inner pan. Bring water in No. 844 pan to boil; cover with No. 845 cover.
3. Steam 30 minutes; add salt pork.
4. Continue steaming 45 minutes.
5. Remove to larger pan; add 2 cups water; allow to simmer 20 minutes.
6. Season to taste.
7. Six servings.

CONSOMMÉ JULIENNE

    ¼ cup string beans, cut into very thin strips
    ¼ cup carrots, cut into very thin strips
    ⅓ cup celery, cut into very thin strips
    1⅓ tablespoons onion, minced fine
    5 cups water
    1 teaspoon salt
    5 chicken bouillon cubes
    ⅛ teaspoon pepper
    2 tablespoons parsley, minced fine

1. Prepare vegetables; bring water to boil in No. 844 pan over medium-high heat; add salt, bouillon. Stir until bouillon is dissolved. Cover; bring to boil.
2. Add finely cut vegetables.
3. Cover; bring to boil; reduce heat to low; cook 15-20 minutes or until vegetables are tender; add pepper.
4. Serve at once very hot. Sprinkle surface with minced parsley.
5. Eight servings.

BORSCH

    1 No. 2 can beets (2½ cups)
    1 teaspoon minced onion
    1 cup condensed bouillon
    1 cup cold water
    ½ teaspoon salt
    1 tablespoon lemon juice
    ¼ cup sour cream

1. Chop beets finely; combine beets, beet juice, onion, bouillon, water.
2. Heat thoroughly, do not boil; add salt, lemon juice.
3. Pour, hot or cold into soup bowls; top with sour cream.
4. Four servings.

GENERAL RECOMMENDATIONS FOR COFFEE

1. Measure coffee accurately.
2. Use freshly drawn water.
3. Serve coffee as soon as possible after brewing.
4. For best results always brew coffee at full capacity of coffee maker.
5. Never boil coffee.
6. Never reuse coffee grounds.
7. Keep coffee maker immaculately clean,
8. Always scald coffee maker before using.

DRIP COFFEE

    Freshly ground coffee
    Freshly boiled water

1. Pour water into kettle; cover; place over <u>high</u> heat until water boils.
2. Place filter in coffee basket; add coffee. Attach coffee basket to water container.
3. Pour boiling water into water container up to desired cup marking.
4. When dripping is completed, remove upper section immediately.
5. Stir brew; serve.

PERCOLATOR COFFEE

    Freshly ground coffee
    Freshly drawn hot water

1. Pour hot water into coffee pot up to desired cup marking.
2. Place coffee basket on stem; add coffee up to desired cup marking; adjust spreader.
3. Place stem and basket in coffee pot; cover.
4. Place over <u>high</u> heat; after perking starts, reduce heat to <u>medium</u>; perk 7-10 minutes.
5. Remove stem and basket immediately.

ICED COFFEE

    16 tablespoons coffee
    3 cups boiling water

1. Make coffee according to directions for drip coffee or percolator coffee.
2. Pour while hot into tall glasses filled with ice cubes.
3. Serve with sugar, cream.
4. Eight servings.

TEA

1. Use water that is fresh and boiling vigorously.
2. Warm teapot by rinsing with hot water.
3. Put a level teaspoon of tea or one tea bag into the teapot for every cup.
4. Pour boiling water on tea; cover.
5. Let tea brew five minutes; stir; serve.

ICED TEA

    1 teaspoon tea leaves or 1 tea bag
    ¾ cup freshly boiling water

1. Place tea, hot water in hot teapot; steep 5 minutes.
2. Pour while hot into tall glass filled with ice cubes.
3. Serve with sugar, lemon or orange slice, sprig of mint.
4. One serving.

COCOA

    3 tablespoons cocoa
    3 tablespoons sugar
    ½ cup water
    2½ cups milk
    ¼ teaspoon salt
    ½ teaspoon vanilla

1. Mix cocoa, sugar; add water; blend; bring to boil over <u>low</u> heat.
2. Add milk, salt; heat over <u>very</u> <u>low</u> heat until scalding hot; remove from heat.
3. Beat with rotary beater; add vanilla.
4. Top with marshmallow.
5. Four servings.

fresh vegetables

772 Pan and Cover

452½ Mixing Bowl

771½ Pan and Cover

771 Pan and Cover

480 Fruit and Vegetable Press

WEAR-EVER NEW METHOD UTENSILS FOR...

fresh vegetables

vegetables

COOKED WITHOUT WATER

General Directions for Fresh Vegetables

1. Select fresh, unwilted vegetables. Clean and remove blemishes.

2. Do not peel vegetables unless special recipe calls for peeling. Then remove only the thinnest possible layer since valuable mineral elements are found directly beneath the skin. It is preferable to scrub vegetables with a stiff brush.

3. Potatoes are usually cooked whole and must be thoroughly dried before cooking. Because of their cellular structure, they require a slightly higher temperature than other vegetables. If cut into halves or quarters to shorten cooking time, place skin side against the utensil, the cut side toward center of the pan.

4. Select utensil food will most nearly fill. The primary cause of vitamin loss during cooking is oxidation. When the pan is full or nearly filled with food, the food has displaced most of the air present and less oxidation takes place. For this reason, fit the food to the pan.

5. Fresh vegetables require only rinsing in cold water before they are cooked. However, vegetables purchased in the market frequently have lost their garden crispness. They may be freshened in cold water 5-10 minutes.

6. Drain vegetables thoroughly before cooking.

7. Cover with specially designed cover; do not remove cover during cooking period. Frequent removal of cover causes loss of moisture and food may scorch.

8. Place over <u>medium</u> heat. When cover is hot to touch—about 5 minutes—reduce heat to <u>low</u>. If it is desirable to hasten the cooking time, change the relative position of the vegetables in the pan once or twice during the cooking operation. This may be done quickly by holding the cover tightly in position with the left hand and shaking the pan with the right hand. However, this is not essential to successful New Method Vegetable Cookery.

9. To cook vegetables on Controlled Heat unit see chart, pages 11, 12.

10. Because most of the natural mineral salts are retained and a fine flavor is developed, New Method vegetables require less seasoning. The seasoning suggested may be altered to suit personal tastes.

11. All vegetables such as potatoes, squash and turnips may be put through the food press.

12. If there is a baby or invalid in the family for whom vegetables must be riced or strained, much time and effort can be saved if these vegetables are cooked along with those for the family, put through the food press while hot, placed in a sterile container and stored in the refrigerator until needed.

General Directions for Quick Frozen Vegetables

1. <u>Do</u> <u>not</u> <u>thaw</u>. Place in vegetable pan in frozen state. If vegetable has been frozen into a solid block, separate into pieces.

2. For one package use No. 771 pan; for two, use No. 771½ pan. Add no water.

3. Cover; place over <u>medium</u> heat 5-8 minutes.

4. Remove cover; turn vegetable over once or twice with large spoon.

5. Replace cover; cook over <u>medium</u> heat until cover is hot to touch—about 5 minutes. Turn vegetable over with spoon once again.

6. Replace cover; when steam escapes, reduce heat to <u>low</u>; cook 5-10 minutes longer.

7. To cook frozen vegetables on Controlled Heat unit see chart, page 12.

ASPARAGUS

1. Snap off lower portion of stalk where it snaps readily. Remove large scales.
2. Put into vegetable pan.
3. Rinse; drain; cover.
4. Place over medium heat until cover is hot to touch—about 5 minutes.
5. Reduce heat to low; cook 15-25 minutes or until tender.
6. Season to taste.

ASPARAGUS AU GRATIN

   1 pound asparagus
   1 cup No. 2 white sauce
   2 tablespoons butter, melted
   ½ cup soft bread crumbs
   1 cup grated American Cheese

1. Prepare, cook asparagus; place in serving dish.
2. Add white sauce.
3. Brown butter, bread crumbs slightly.
4. Spread over asparagus; sprinkle with cheese.
5. Four servings.

ARTICHOKES

1. Remove stem, outer leaves.
2. Put into vegetable pan; freshen in cold water 30 minutes.
3. Rinse; drain; cover.
4. Place over medium heat until cover is hot to touch—about 5 minutes.
5. Reduce heat to low; cook 30-45 minutes.
6. Cut out choke.
7. Season; serve with melted butter or Hollandaise sauce.

BEANS, GREEN OR YELLOW

1. Wash well; snap ends; string, if necessary; cut.
2. Put into vegetable pan.
3. Rinse; drain; cover.
4. Place over medium heat until cover is hot to touch—about 5 minutes.
5. Reduce heat to low; cook 30-35 minutes or until tender.
6. Season to taste.

BEANS, LIMA

1. Shell; wash; discard bad beans.
2. Put into vegetable pan.
3. Rinse; drain; cover.
4. Place over medium heat until cover is hot to touch—about 5 minutes.
5. Reduce heat to low; cook 25-30 minutes or until tender.
6. Season to taste.

BEETS

1. Remove roots, stems, blemishes; scrub with stiff brush; slice, dice or leave whole if small.
2. Put into vegetable pan.
3. Rinse; drain; cover.
4. Place over medium heat until cover is hot to touch—about 5 minutes.
5. Reduce heat to low; cook 30-35 minutes if sliced or diced; if whole, 35-40 minutes or until tender.

HARVARD BEETS

   2 pounds beets
   1 tablespoon cornstarch
   ½ cup sugar
   ¼ cup water
   ½ cup lemon juice or vinegar
   ½ teaspoon salt

1. Prepare, cook beets.
2. Mix cornstarch, sugar, water, lemon juice, salt together; cook 5 minutes.
3. Pour over cooked beets; allow to stand a few minutes before serving.
4. Six servings.

BEET GREENS

1. Wash carefully; remove wilted leaves.
2. Put into vegetable pan.
3. Rinse; drain; cover.
4. Place over medium heat until cover is hot to touch—about 5 minutes.
5. Reduce heat to low; cook 12-15 minutes or until tender.
6. Season to taste.

BROCCOLI

1. Select stalks with dark green buds; remove tough outer leaves and stems; cut into moderate size pieces; wash.
2. Put into vegetable pan; stems, leaves in bottom, flowers on top.
3. Rinse; drain; cover.
4. Place over medium heat until cover is hot to touch—about 5 minutes.
5. Reduce heat to low; cook 25-30 minutes or until tender.
6. Season; serve with melted butter, Hollandaise, white or rarebit sauce.

BRUSSELS SPROUTS

1. Wash; remove defective leaves.
2. Put into vegetable pan; freshen in cold water 30 minutes.
3. Rinse; drain; cover.
4. Place over medium heat until cover is hot to touch—about 5 minutes.
5. Reduce heat to low; cook 25-30 minutes or until tender.
6. Season to taste.

CABBAGE

1. Remove wilted leaves; wash; quarter; core; chop or shred.
2. Put into vegetable pan.
3. Rinse; drain; cover.
4. Place over medium heat until cover is hot to touch—about 5 minutes.
5. Reduce heat to low; cook 20-25 minutes or until tender.
6. Season to taste.

CARROTS

1. Remove tip of root, stem, blemishes; wash, scrub with stiff brush; slice, dice or leave whole.
2. Put into vegetable pan.
3. Rinse; drain; cover.
4. Place over medium heat until cover is hot to touch—about 5 minutes.
5. Reduce heat to low; cook 18 minutes if sliced or diced; if whole 25-30 minutes or until tender.
6. Season to taste.

CAULIFLOWER

1. Select a white head heavy for its size with fresh green leaves.
2. Remove leaves; cut off stalks; score core of plant with six crisscross cuts if to be cooked whole or separate into flowerets.
3. Wash well; freshen in cold water 30 minutes.
4. Put into vegetable pan; leaves, stalk in bottom, flowerets on top.
5. Rinse; drain; cover.
6. Place over medium heat until cover is hot to touch—about 5 minutes.
7. Reduce heat to low; cook 20 minutes if separated into flowerets; 25 minutes if whole.
8. Season to taste.

CELERY

1. Trim root; separate stalks; remove leaves, blemishes; wash well; dice.
2. Put into vegetable pan.
3. Rinse; drain; cover.
4. Place over medium heat until cover is hot to touch—about 5 minutes.
5. Reduce heat to low; cook 20-25 minutes or until tender.
6. Season to taste.

CORN ON THE COB

1. Select young tender ears; remove husks, silk, bad spots.
2. Wash corn, inner husks.
3. Make bed of inner husks in bottom of vegetable pan. Place corn on bed in layers, sprinkling each layer with salt; cover.
4. Place over medium heat until cover is hot to touch—about 5 minutes.
5. Reduce heat to low; cook 12-15 minutes or until tender.

EGGPLANT

1. Pare; cut into ¼ inch slices.
2. Dip into batter or not as desired.
3. Melt shortening in No. 940 pan over medium heat; add eggplant; brown on both sides; cook until tender.
4. Season to taste.

KALE

1. Cut off roots, heavy part of leaf; discard wilted leaves; wash well.
2. Put into vegetable pan.
3. Rinse; drain; cover.
4. Place over medium heat until cover is hot to touch—about 5 minutes.
5. Reduce heat to low; cook 18-20 minutes or until tender.
6. Chop fine; season to taste.

KOHLRABI

1. Select small pale green bulbs; cut off tops; scrub; slice or quarter.
2. Put into vegetable pan.
3. Rinse; drain; cover.
4. Place over medium heat until cover is hot to touch—about 5 minutes.
5. Reduce heat to low; cook 25-30 minutes or until tender.
6. Season to taste.

CREAMED MUSHROOMS

    1 pound mushrooms, 18-25 mushrooms
    5 tablespoons butter, melted
    ½ teaspoon salt
    1½ tablespoons flour
    ½ cup thin cream

1. Wash mushrooms; slice thinly.
2. Put into vegetable pan.
3. Rinse; drain; cover.
4. Cook over medium heat 4 minutes.
5. Drain; add butter, salt.
6. Stir in flour; add cream.
7. Cook 5 minutes; stirring constantly.
8. Season with grated nutmeg.
9. Six servings.

MUSHROOMS

1. Wash mushrooms; remove tip of stem; leave whole or slice.
2. Put into vegetable pan.
3. Rinse; drain; cover.
4. Place over medium heat until cover is hot to touch—about 5 minutes.
5. Reduce heat to low; cook 10 minutes if sliced; 15 minutes if whole.
6. Season to taste.

ONIONS

1. Remove onion skins under cold water.
2. Put into vegetable pan.
3. Rinse; drain; cover.
4. Place over medium heat until cover is hot to touch—about 5 minutes.
5. Reduce heat to low; cook 25-30 minutes or until tender.
6. Season; serve with melted butter or white sauce.

PARSNIPS

1. Remove stem end, root tip; wash.
2. Put into vegetable pan.
3. Rinse; drain; cover.
4. Place over medium heat until cover is hot to touch—about 5 minutes.
5. Reduce heat to low; cook 30-35 minutes or until tender.
6. Plunge parsnips into cold water; remove skins; cut into halves.
7. Melt shortening in No. 940 pan.
8. Add parsnips; brown on all sides.
9. Season to taste.

PEAS

1. Shell peas; wash.
2. Put into vegetable pan.
3. Rinse; drain; cover.
4. Place over medium heat until cover is hot to touch—about 5 minutes.
5. Reduce heat to low; cook 15-18 minutes or until tender.
6. Season; serve with melted butter or white sauce.

BAKED POTATOES

1. Scrub potatoes with stiff brush; remove blemishes. Make a crisscross cut on flat side; dry.
2. Preheat vegetable pan over medium-high heat 5 minutes.
3. Put potatoes into heated pan; cover.
4. Reduce heat to medium 10 minutes.
5. Reduce heat to medium-low 40-45 minutes or until done.
6. Press lightly on baked potato to open crisscross slit. Add 1 teaspoon butter, dash of paprika, salt to each. Or if desired, sprinkle opening with grated cheese, chopped parsley.

CANDIED SWEET POTATOES

6 medium sweet potatoes
1 cup brown sugar
1½ teaspoons salt
⅛ teaspoon pepper
6 tablespoons butter

1. Scrub potatoes with stiff brush; remove blemishes; slice crosswise.
2. Put into No. 940 pan.
3. Mix brown sugar, seasonings; sprinkle over sweet potatoes. Dot with butter; cover.
4. Place over low heat; cook 30 minutes.
5. Remove cover; increase heat to medium last 5 minutes to thicken syrup. Turn potatoes to glaze.
6. Eight servings.

GEORGIAN SWEET POTATOES

2 pounds sweet potatoes
4 tablespoons butter
1 teaspoon salt
Hot milk to moisten
4 tablespoons molasses
1 teaspoon butter

1. Scrub sweet potatoes with stiff brush; remove blemishes. Dry; cut in half.
2. Put into vegetable pan; cover.
3. Place over medium heat until cover is hot to touch—about 5 minutes.
4. Reduce heat to low; cook 30-45 minutes or until tender.
5. Remove from pan to food press; rice.
6. To riced potatoes add butter, salt, hot milk; beat until smooth.
7. Put into greased No. 802 pan.
8. Boil molasses, butter together; pour over sweet potatoes.
9. Heat thoroughly over low heat.
10. Eight servings.

MASHED POTATOES

1. Cook; rice potatoes.
2. To 4 cups riced potatoes, add ½ cup hot milk, 1 tablespoon butter, ½ teaspoon salt.
3. Beat until light; fluffy.
4. Four servings.

RICED POTATOES

1. Place one or two baked potatoes in press at a time. Remove any dry crust before ricing; if creamy yellow color is not desirable, skin potatoes before ricing.
2. Place roller in cone, with top of roller in the palm of the hand. Do not grasp it or hold it firm. With a roller motion press against sides of ricer.
3. Add salt with each addition of potatoes.
4. If potatoes stick to the roller, press it firmly against cone, turning roller at one place against cone until food is released from roller.
5. Remove food left on outside of cone by scraping with a wooden spoon.
6. Cut butter into cubes, place on top of riced potatoes, preferably before last potatoes are riced.
7. Rice potatoes into a warm dish or bowl.
8. Serve at once.

PUMPKIN

1. Wash; halve; remove seeds, fiber. Cut into two-inch pieces; do not peel.
2. Put into vegetable pan, skin side down, placing one on top of the other; cover.
3. Place over medium heat until cover is hot to touch—about 5 minutes.
4. Reduce heat to low; cook 35-45 minutes or until tender.
5. Put through food press; use for pie or as desired.

RUTABAGA

1. Remove tops, roots; pare thinly; dice.
2. Put into vegetable pan.
3. Rinse; drain; cover.
4. Place over medium heat until cover is hot to touch—about 5 minutes.
5. Reduce heat to low; cook 30-35 minutes or until tender.
6. Season to taste.

SPINACH

1. Remove roots, tough stems; discard wilted leaves; wash carefully.
2. Put into vegetable pan.
3. Rinse; drain; cover.
4. Place over medium heat until cover is hot to touch—about 5 minutes.
5. Reduce heat to low; cook 10-15 minutes or until tender.
6. Drain; chop fine if desired.
7. For variety, serve with vinegar and hard cooked eggs.

SPINACH AND BACON

    2 pounds spinach
    ¾ teaspoon salt
    ¼ pound lean bacon, diced
    ¼ cup chopped onion

1. Clean, wash, drain spinach.
2. Put into vegetable pan.
3. Rinse; drain; cover.
4. Place over medium heat until cover is hot to touch—about 5 minutes.
5. Reduce heat to low; cook 10 minutes.
6. Season with salt.
7. Place bacon in No. 940 pan; cook until crisp.
8. Remove bacon; add onion; cook 5 minutes.
9. Pour onion, bacon fat over spinach; mix well.
10. Garnish with bacon.
11. Four servings.

SQUASH, SUMMER

1. Wash; quarter; dice.
2. Put into vegetable pan.
3. Rinse; drain; cover.
4. Place over medium heat until cover is hot to touch—about 5 minutes.
5. Reduce heat to low; cook 10-20 minutes or until tender.
6. Season to taste.

SQUASH, WINTER

1. Wash; halve; remove seeds, fiber; if large, cut into quarters or eighths.
2. Put into vegetable pan, skin side down, placing one on the other.
3. Rinse; drain; cover.
4. Place over medium heat until cover is hot to touch—about 5 minutes.
5. Reduce heat to low; cook 20-25 minutes or until tender.
6. If desired, put through food press.
7. Season to taste.

SWISS CHARD

1. Remove wilted leaves; wash, cut.
2. Put into vegetable pan.
3. Rinse; drain; cover.
4. Place over medium heat until cover is hot to touch—about 5 minutes.
5. Reduce heat to low; cook 10-15 minutes or until tender.
6. Chop fine if desired; season to taste.

TOMATOES

1. Wash; remove blemishes; quarter.
2. Put into vegetable pan; cover.
3. Place over medium heat until cover is hot to touch—about 5 minutes.
4. Reduce heat to low; cook 10-15 minutes or until soft.
5. Season to taste; soft bread crumbs may be added.

STUFFED TOMATOES

    8 medium sized tomatoes
    3 cups soft bread (5 small slices)
    2 tablespoons minced onion
    2 tablespoons minced green pepper
    2 teaspoons salt
    1/8 teaspoon pepper

1. Select well shaped, firm tomatoes; wash; cut slice from top about one-fourth inch thick. With teaspoon loosen, remove center, leaving solid shell unbroken.
2. Prepare bread by pulling it into small pieces; add tomato pulp, onion, green pepper, seasonings; mix.
3. Fill tomato shells; put into vegetable pan; cover.
4. Place over medium heat until cover is hot to touch—about 5 minutes.
5. Reduce heat to low; cook 20 minutes.
6. Tomatoes should have firm whole appearance when done. Remove from pan, using two spoons so as not to break or spill tomato.
7. Sprinkle top with buttered bread crumbs; top each tomato with small sprig of parsley.
8. Eight servings.

TURNIPS

1. Remove tops, roots; scrub with stiff brush; slice or dice.
2. Put into vegetable pan.
3. Rinse; drain; cover.
4. Place over medium heat until cover is hot to touch—about 5 minutes.
5. Reduce heat to low; cook 35-45 minutes or until tender.
6. Season to taste.

HOT POTATO SALAD

    6 medium potatoes
    4 slices bacon, diced
    1/4 cup minced onion
    1 egg, well beaten
    4 tablespoons vinegar
    1 1/2 teaspoons salt
    2 hard cooked eggs

1. Scrub potatoes with vegetable brush.
2. Dry; score each end with crisscross cut.
3. Preheat vegetable pan over medium-high heat 5 minutes.
4. Put potatoes into heated pan; cover.
5. Reduce heat to medium 10 minutes.
6. Reduce heat to medium-low 40-45 minutes.
7. Remove thin outside skin from potatoes; slice while hot.
8. Broil diced bacon in No. 940 pan; cook onion in bacon fat until tender; drain off fat.
9. Add bacon, onion to potatoes; toss.
10. Slowly add beaten egg to fat; add vinegar, salt. Pour over potatoes; mix.
11. Return salad to No. 940 pan; cover.
12. Place over low heat 10-15 minutes.
13. Serve hot, garnished with sieved, hard cooked eggs.
14. Eight servings.

SAUCES

SAUCES USED WITH VEGETABLES

White Sauce No. 1
For Cream Soups

- 1 tablespoon butter
- 1 tablespoon flour
- ¼ teaspoon salt
- 1 cup milk

1. Melt butter; add flour, seasoning.
2. Stir until well blended. Add milk gradually, stirring constantly.
3. Bring to boiling point; boil 2 minutes.

White Sauce No. 2
For Vegetables and Fish

- 2 tablespoons butter
- 2 tablespoons flour
- ¼ teaspoon salt
- 1 cup milk

Follow directions for White Sauce No. 1.

White Sauce No. 3
For Soufflés and Croquettes

- 3 tablespoons butter
- 3 tablespoons flour
- ¼ teaspoon salt
- 1 cup milk

Follow directions for White Sauce No. 1.

Drawn Butter Sauce
For Vegetables and Fish

- ⅓ cup butter
- 3 tablespoons flour
- 1½ cups hot water or fish stock
- 1 teaspoon lemon juice

Follow directions for White Sauce No. 1.

HOLLANDAISE SAUCE

- 2 egg yolks
- ½ teaspoon salt
- Dash cayenne pepper
- ½ cup melted butter or margarine
- 1 tablespoon lemon juice

1. Beat egg yolks until thick; add salt, pepper.
2. Add 3 tablespoons melted butter, a little at a time, beating constantly.
3. Slowly beat in remaining butter alternately with lemon juice.
4. Serve with green vegetables.
5. Six servings.

RAREBIT SAUCE

- 1 bouillon cube
- 1 cup boiling water
- ¼ cup butter or margarine
- ¼ cup flour
- 1 cup milk
- 1 teaspoon dry mustard
- 1 teaspoon Worcestershire sauce
- ½ pound (2 cups) grated American cheese

1. Dissolve bouillon cube in boiling water.
2. Melt butter in vegetable pan over very low heat; add flour; stir until smooth.
3. Gradually add milk, bouillon; cook, stirring constantly until smooth, thick.
4. Add mustard, Worcestershire sauce, cheese; stir until cheese is melted.
5. Six servings.

VEGETABLE BUYING GUIDE

Vegetable	Characteristics of Good Quality	Number of Servings	Amount to Buy	Pan to Use
Asparagus	Stalks straight, crisp, green; tips moist, compact, unbroken	2 4 6	⅔ pound; 8–10 stalks 1 ⅓ pounds; 16–20 stalks 2 pounds; 24–30 stalks	771 771 ½ 772
Beans, Green or Yellow	Pods crisp, bright color, well filled	2 4 6	½ pound 1 pound 1 ½ pounds	770 ½ 771 771 ½
Beans, Lima	Pods clean, unspotted, green, well filled	2 4 6	1–1 ½ pounds in pod 2–3 pounds in pod 4 pounds in pod	770 ½ 771 771 ½
Beets	Young, tops fresh, unwilted; mature; smooth velvety skin	2 4 6	½ pound; 2–4 beets 1 pound; 4–8 beets 1 ½ pounds; 6–12 beets	770 ½ 771 771 ½
Broccoli	Buds dark green, compact; stems short, crisp	2 4 6	⅔ pound 1 ⅓ pounds 2 pounds	771 771 ½ 772
Brussels Sprouts	Heads round, solid, compact, green	2 4 6	½ pound 1 pound 1 ½ pounds; 1 quart	770 ½ 771 771 ½
Cabbage	Head solid, heavy; leaves fresh	2 4 6	½ pound 1 pound 1 ½ pounds	771 771 ½ 772
Carrots	Firm, uniform shape; bright color; fresh tops	2 4 6	⅔ pound 1 ⅓ pounds 2 pounds	771 771 ½ 772
Cauliflower	Head white, well filled; leaves fresh, green	2 4 6	small; 1 pound medium; 1 ½ pounds large; 2 ½ pounds	771 ½ 772 774 ½
Corn on Cob	Ears well filled; husks green; kernels soft, milky	2 4	2–4 ears 4–8 ears	772 774 ½
Greens, Kale, Spinach, Swiss Chard	Leaves fresh, crisp, tender	2 4 6	¾ pound 1 ½ pounds 2 ½ pounds	771 ½ 772 774 ½
Peas	Pods green, unspotted, velvety, well filled	2 4 6	1 pound 2 pounds 3 pounds	770 ½ 771 771 ½
Potatoes	Clean, smooth, firm. Regular shape and size	2 4 6	2 medium; ⅔ pound 4 medium; 1 ⅓ pounds 6 medium; 2 pounds	771 771 ½ 772
Squash, Summer (Cymling, Crookneck, Straightneck, Vegetable marrow)	Young, firm, thin skinned	2 4 6	small; ½ pound medium; 1 pound large; 1 ½ pounds	770 ½ 771 771 ½
Squash, Winter (Hubbard, Acorn)	Thin skinned; heavy for size	2 4	1 acorn; ¼ Hubbard 2 acorn; ½ Hubbard	771 ½ 774 ½
Turnips and Rutabagas	Roots smooth, firm, heavy; size small to medium	2 4 6	⅔ pound 1 ⅓ pounds 2 pounds	770 ½ 771 771 ½

fresh fruits

770½ 771
771½ 772 773 774½ Pans and Covers

480 Fruit and Vegetable Press

452½ Mixing Bowl

WEAR-EVER NEW METHOD UTENSILS FOR...

fresh
fruits

fruits

General Directions for Fruits

1. Select fresh, ripe, unspotted fruit.
2. Wash well; remove stems and blemishes.
3. Follow recipe. Do not core or peel unless recipe so directs.
4. Put into pan. Best results are obtained when pan is full. Cover.
5. Place over medium heat until cover is hot to touch—about 5 minutes.
6. Reduce heat to low; cook until done.
7. To cook fruits on Controlled Heat unit see chart, page 12.
8. To make sauce, put through food press.

General Directions for Berries

1. Select ripe, well colored berries free from white, green or off-color tips.
2. Remove spoiled berries; put into food press; wash by letting water run over them; stem or hull.
3. Proceed according to instructions 4, 5, 6, 7, 8 given above for Fruits.

APPLE SAUCE

1. Wash apples; remove stems, blemishes; quarter; do not core.
2. Put into pan; cover.
3. Place over medium heat until cover is hot to touch—about 5 minutes.
4. Reduce heat to low; cook 10-15 minutes or until soft.
5. Add sugar to taste; cook 5 minutes.
6. Put through food press.

BAKED APPLES

1. Wash; remove cores, blemishes.
2. Score around middle, just enough to cut skin.
3. Put into pan; fill center of each with 1 tablespoon sugar mixed with ¼ teaspoon cinnamon or favorite filling.
4. Make syrup of 4 tablespoons butter, 1 cup sugar, 1 tablespoon water; pour over apples; cover.
5. Place over low heat; cook 30-40 minutes or until tender.

STUFFED APPLES

1. Prepare apples as for baking.
2. Place in pan; fill cavities with chopped dates, raisins; a combination of crushed pineapple, raisins; orange marmalade; jam; cover.
3. Place over low heat; cook 30-40 minutes or until tender.

GRILLED APPLE RINGS

1. Wash; core large cooking apples.
2. Slice into one-half inch thick rings.
3. Dip into flour; broil in 2 tablespoons butter in No. 940 pan.
4. Serve with pork chops or sausage.

CINNAMON APPLES

1. Wash apples; peel thinly; core; quarter.
2. Put into pan; cover.
3. Place over medium heat until cover is hot to touch—about 5 minutes.
4. Reduce heat to low; cook 10 minutes or until just tender.
5. Add ¼ cup cinnamon drops and sugar disolved in ¼ cup water.
6. Cover; cook 5 minutes longer.

GLAZED BANANAS

 6 large, firm, ripe bananas
 3 tablespoons lemon juice
 1 cup sugar
 4 tablespoons butter

1. Peel bananas; cut into halves lengthwise.
2. Roll bananas in lemon juice, then in sugar.
3. Melt butter in No. 940 pan over medium heat.
4. Put bananas into pan; reduce heat to medium low; sauté bananas basting constantly until golden brown.
5. Serve hot with meat or fish.

CRANBERRY JELLY

1. Pick over cranberries; wash; drain.
2. Put into pan; cover.
3. Place over low heat; cook 25-30 minutes or until soft.
4. Put through food press. Return to pan; add 1 cup sugar for each pound berries used.
5. Cover; cook 5 minutes; mold.

CRANBERRY SAUCE

1. Pick over 4 cups cranberries. Wash; drain.
2. Put into pan; cover.
3. Place over low heat; cook 15-20 minutes or until soft.
4. Add 2 cups sugar; cook 5 minutes.
5. Put through food press; mold.

GLAZED CRANBERRIES

 3 cups cranberries
 1 cup sugar
 ¼ cup water
 1 orange put through food chopper
 1 lemon put through food chopper

1. Put cranberries into food press cone. Wash, discard soft or bad berries.
2. Put sugar, water into vegetable pan; bring to boil over high heat; reduce heat to medium; boil 4-5 minutes until syrup is thick.
3. Add cranberries; reduce heat to low 2-3 minutes until juice starts to come from berries; turn heat to medium; cook 3-4 minutes until cranberries start to burst.
4. Remove from heat; add orange, lemon.
5. Mix well, being careful not to crush fruit. Chill.
6. Six servings.

PEARS

1. Wash pears; peel thinly; core; quarter.
2. Put into pan; cover.
3. Place over <u>medium</u> heat until cover is hot to touch—about 5 minutes.
4. Reduce heat to <u>low</u>; cook 20-25 minutes.
5. Add sugar to taste.
6. Serve as dessert or breakfast fruit.

SPICED PEACHES

>6 peaches
>12 whole cloves
>½ cup brown sugar
>3 tablespoons butter
>2 tablespoons lemon juice
>Grated rind of one lemon
>1 inch cinnamon stick

1. Dip peaches into scalding water for one minute. Remove skins; halve; take out stones.
2. Put into pan. Insert a clove into each half.
3. Sprinkle with sugar; dot with butter; add lemon juice, rind, cinnamon stick; cover.
4. Place over <u>low</u> heat; cook 20-25 minutes or until tender.
5. Serve as garnish with meat.

MINTED PEACHES

>1 No. 2½ can peach halves
>2 teaspoons butter
>Mint jelly

1. Open can of peaches; drain well in food press.
2. Melt butter in No. 940 pan over <u>medium</u>-<u>low</u> heat.
3. When butter is melted, put drained peaches in pan; brown lightly on both sides.
4. When peaches are browned, remove to piece of absorbent paper; turn cup side up; cool 2-3 minutes.
5. Place one teaspoon mint jelly in center of each peach.
6. Serve with roast lamb.
7. Six servings.

SPICED APRICOT GOBLINS

>1 No. 2 can spiced apricots
>Whole cloves
>Water cress or lettuce hearts

1. Empty contents of can into vegetable pan.
2. Simmer over <u>low</u> heat.
3. Drain off juice.
4. Insert whole cloves in apricots to form goblin faces, using one each for eyes, one for nose, 5-6 in half moon for the mouth.
5. Serve on water cress or in lettuce cups around roast fresh ham.
6. Six servings.

CINNAMON PINEAPPLE RINGS

>2 tablespoons red cinnamon candies
>½ cup juice from pineapple
>6 slices canned pineapple

1. Dissolve red cinnamon candies in pineapple juice. Pour over pineapple slices; let stand 3-4 hours.
2. Drain onto absorbent paper.
3. Melt 1 tablespoon fat in No. 940 pan; place pineapple slices in pan. Brown over <u>medium</u>-<u>high</u> heat 2-3 minutes on one side; turn; brown on the other.
4. Serve with broiled ham slice.
5. Six servings.

APRICOT SAUCE

>2 cups dried apricots
>1 cup water
>Sugar

1. Wash apricots thoroughly; drain.
2. Follow directions for dried fruit.
3. Remove from steamer plate. Put through food press. Sweeten to taste.
4. Eight servings.

PARADISE SAUCE

    4 cups cranberries
    6-7 apples
    2 cups sugar

1. Pick over cranberries; wash; drain.
2. Put into pan; cover.
3. Place over low heat; cook 15-20 minutes.
4. Put through food press. Return to pan; add sliced apples
5. Cook gently until apples are soft but still retain their shape. Add sugar; cook 5 minutes longer.

FRESH FRUIT SAUCE

    1 quart peaches, cut into small pieces
    or
    1 quart berries
    1 cup sugar

1. Wash fruit; put into pan; add sugar; cover.
2. Place over medium heat; cook 7-10 minutes.
3. Serve over desserts.

RHUBARB SAUCE

1. Remove tops; wash; cut into pieces.
2. Put into pan; cover.
3. Place over medium heat until cover is hot to touch—about 5 minutes.
4. Reduce heat to low; cook 15 minutes.
5. Sweeten to taste; cook 5 more minutes.
6. Serve as dessert.

STRAWBERRY—RHUBARB SAUCE

    1 pint strawberries
    ½ pound pink rhubarb
    ½ cup sugar

1. Wash; hull strawberries.
2. Wash; dice rhubarb.
3. Combine fruit, sugar; put into pan; cover.
4. Place over medium heat until cover is hot to touch—about 5 minutes.
5. Reduce heat to low; cook 10 minutes.
6. Serve over ice cream or cottage pudding.

FRUIT BUYING GUIDE

Fruit	Characteristics of Quality	Number of Servings	Amount to Buy	Pan to Use
Apples	Flesh firm; color bright	6	2 pounds	772
Cranberries	Firm; not overripe	6-12	1 pound or 1 quart	772
Peaches	Flesh firm; color bright	6	6 medium or 1 ½ pounds	772
Pears	Flesh firm; color bright	6	6 medium or 1 ½–2 pounds	772
Rhubarb	Stalks thick, crisp; color bright	6	2 pounds	772

dried foods and puddings

845 Cover

801 Inset Pans

817 Steamer Plate

802 Inner Pan

807 Ring

843 Cover

844 Pan

WEAR-EVER NEW METHOD UTENSILS FOR...

dried foods and puddings

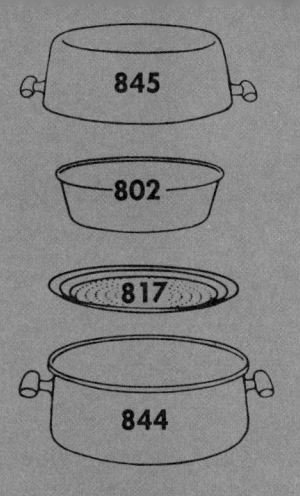

For steamed dried foods and puddings.

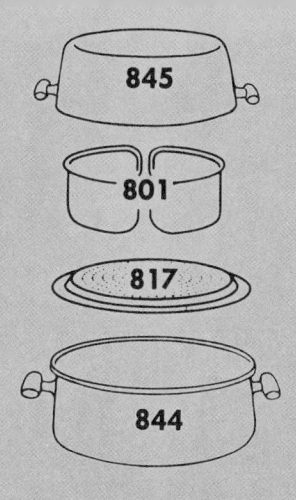

For two steamed dried foods or puddings at one time.

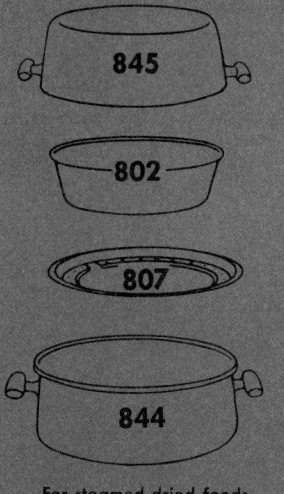

For steamed dried foods and puddings.

For steamed dried foods and puddings.

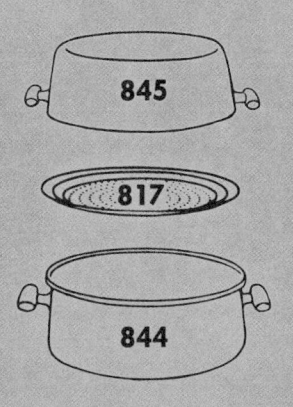

For steamed dried foods; for reheating food.

WEAR-EVER

New Method Utensils can be used in many combinations, thus increasing their usefulness.

45

dried foods and puddings

General Directions for Cooking Cereals

1. Place 1 quart water in No. 844 pan; bring to boil. If desired, add one tablespoon cream of tartar or vinegar to this water to prevent discoloration of utensil.
2. Put required water (see chart below) in No. 802 pan; add salt; bring to boil.
3. Add cereal gradually to boiling water, stirring constantly.
4. Place No. 807 ring in No. 844 pan.
5. Place No. 802 pan on ring; cover with No. 843 cover.
6. Place over <u>high</u> heat until steam first escapes beneath cover.
7. Reduce heat to <u>low</u>; cook required time. See chart below.
8. To cook cereals on Controlled Heat unit see chart, page 13.
9. Dried fruits such as raisins, dates, apricots, peaches, prunes or figs may be added for variety and additional nutritive value. These should be carefully washed and added one-half hour before cereal is done.

CEREAL TIME TABLE

Cereal	Quantity	Water	Salt	Time
Rolled Oats	1 cup	2 cups	1 tsp.	30 minutes
Rolled Rye or Wheat	1 cup	2 cups	1 tsp.	25 minutes
Rice	1 cup	2½ cups	1 tsp.	35 minutes
Corn Meal	½ cup	2 cups	½ tsp.	2½ hours
Fine Wheat Breakfast Foods	½ cup	2 cups	½ tsp.	30 minutes
Oatmeal (coarse)	½ cup	2 cups	½ tsp.	3 hours
Hominy	½ cup	2 cups	½ tsp.	1 hour
Cracked Whole Wheat	½ cup	2 cups	½ tsp.	3 hours

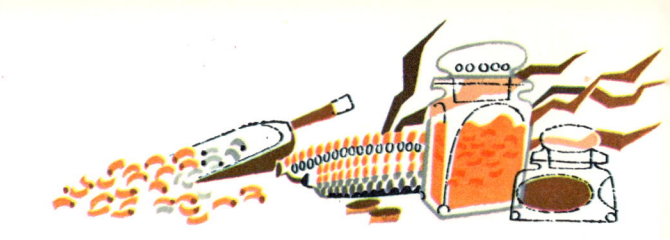

General Directions for Cooking Dried Vegetables

1. Wash well; put into No. 802 pan; cover with two parts cold water for one part vegetable; soak overnight.
2. Place 1 quart water in No. 844 pan; bring to boil. If desired, add one tablespoon cream of tartar or vinegar to this water to prevent discoloration of utensil.
3. Place No. 807 ring in No. 844 pan. Place No. 802 pan containing vegetable and water in which vegetable was soaked on ring; cover with No. 843 cover.
4. Place over <u>high</u> heat until steam first escapes beneath cover.
5. Reduce heat to <u>low</u>; cook 1-2 hours or until vegetable is tender.
6. To cook dried vegetables on Controlled Heat unit see chart, page 13.
7. If desired, vegetables may be steamed over a roast instead of water. Brown meat first; adjust ring and No. 802 pan containing vegetable and water; cover. Control heat as for the roast.

DRIED LIMA BEANS

1½ cups dried lima beans
2 tablespoons butter
1 teaspoon salt
⅛ teaspoon pepper

1. Prepare lima beans, soaked overnight, according to directions for dried vegetables; cook 1-2 hours.
2. Season with butter, salt, pepper.

CORN PUDDING

3 cups crushed canned corn
1 cup milk
1 teaspoon grated onion
1 egg, slightly beaten
1 teaspoon salt
Dash of pepper
¼ green pepper, diced
½ pimiento, diced
3 tablespoons butter

1. Combine crushed corn, milk, onion, egg, salt, pepper. Mix well.
2. Butter No. 802 pan. Pour corn mixture into pan. Sprinkle diced green pepper, pimiento over top. Stir just enough to distribute them through mixture. Dot top with butter.

3. Place 1 quart boiling water in bottom of No. 844 pan; adjust steamer ring; place pan on ring; cover; steam 1½ hours.
4. Six servings.

BAKED BEANS

2 cups navy beans
4 slices bacon
1 tablespoon salt
4 tablespoons molasses
2 cups canned tomatoes

1. Wash beans; soak overnight; steam according to directions for dried vegetables, placing strips of bacon over beans; cook 1-2 hours.
2. Add salt, molasses.
3. Put tomatoes through food press.
4. Pour tomatoes over beans. (Do not pour off liquid in which beans have been cooked.)
5. Remove water from No. 844 pan. Pour in bean mixture; cover.
6. Place over <u>simmer</u> heat; cook 7-8 hours; add more tomato juice if mixture becomes dry.
7. Six servings.

General Directions for Cooking Dried Fruits

1. Place 1 quart water in No. 844 pan; bring to boil. If desired, add one tablespoon cream of tartar or vinegar to this water to prevent discoloration of utensil.
2. Wash dried fruit; put into No. 802 pan; cover with one part cold water for two parts fruit.
3. Place No. 807 ring in No. 844 pan.
4. Place No. 802 pan on ring; cover with No. 843 cover.
5. Place over <u>high</u> heat until steam first escapes beneath cover.
6. Reduce heat to <u>low</u>; cook 30 minutes or until tender; add sugar.
7. To cook dried fruits on Controlled Heat unit see chart, page 13.
8. If desired, fruits may be steamed over a roast instead of water. Brown meat first; adjust ring and No. 802 pan containing fruit and water in No. 844 pan; cover. Control heat as for the roast.
9. Steamed dried fruits may be served as breakfast fruit or combined with cereals. They also provide the basis for many delicious puddings, fruit and upside-down cakes. They also can be prepared as sauces to be served over puddings and cakes.

General Directions for Cooking Macaroni, Spaghetti and Noodles

1. Place 1 quart water in No. 844 pan; bring to boil. If desired, add 1 tablespoon cream of tartar or vinegar to this water to prevent discoloration of utensil.
2. Put macaroni, spaghetti or noodles into No. 802 pan; add two parts boiling water for one part food. Place No. 807 ring in No. 844 pan.
3. Place No. 802 pan on ring; cover with No. 843 cover.
4. Place over <u>high</u> heat until steam first escapes beneath cover.
5. Reduce heat to <u>low</u>; cook 30 minutes.
6. To cook on Controlled Heat unit see chart, page 13.
7. Drain; use as directed in recipe.

TAMALE RICE WITH FRANKFURTERS

    2 tablespoons shortening
    1 onion, chopped
    2 tablespoons vinegar
    2 tablespoons brown sugar
    1 tablespoon lemon juice
    1 cup ketchup
    1 cup stock or water
    2 teaspoons salt
    1 tablespoon Worcestershire sauce
    3 cups cooked rice
    6 frankfurters

1. Melt shortening in No. 940 pan; add onion; brown.
2. Add vinegar, brown sugar, lemon juice, ketchup, stock, salt, Worcestershire sauce; cover; simmer 15 minutes.
3. Grease No. 802 pan; add cooked rice.
4. Pour onion, liquid mixture over rice; stir until mixed; arrange frankfurters on top.
5. Place one quart boiling water in bottom of No. 844 pan; adjust steamer ring; place pan on ring; cover; steam 40 minutes.
6. Six servings.

TALLARENE

    3 tablespoons butter
    1 medium size onion, minced
    1 pound ground beef
    1½ cups tomato soup
    1 cup cold water
    1 teaspoon salt
    2 cups uncooked broad noodles
    2 cups whole grain corn
    1 cup grated cheese

1. Melt butter in No. 940 pan; add onion; cook over <u>low</u> heat until tender.
2. Add meat; cook until brown.
3. Add tomato soup, water, salt, noodles, corn. Mix; cover; cook slowly 10 minutes.
4. Pour into No. 802 pan; sprinkle with cheese. Place one quart boiling water in bottom of No. 844 pan; adjust steamer ring; place pan on ring; cover; steam 45 minutes.
5. Eight servings.

AMERICAN SPAGHETTI

    1 9-ounce package spaghetti
    1 slice ham, cut into 1 inch pieces
    ½ pound sharp cheese, grated
    1 tablespoon butter
    2½ cups canned tomatoes
    1 green pepper, chopped fine
    1 onion, chopped fine
    Salt, pepper
    1 cup cooked mushrooms

1. Steam spaghetti as directed.
2. Brown ham in No. 940 pan.
3. Lift out ham; add cheese, butter; stir until melted.
4. Add tomatoes, green pepper, onion to cheese mixture.
5. Cover; cook over <u>low</u> heat 10 minutes.
6. Season; add mushrooms, ham.
7. Bring to boil, stirring constantly.
8. Place spaghetti on platter; top with sauce; sprinkle with grated cheese.

BAKED MACARONI, HAM AND CHEESE

    6 tablespoons butter
    ½ cup flour
    1 quart hot milk
    2 teaspoons salt
    ⅛ teaspoon cayenne pepper
    4 cups cooked macaroni
    1½ pounds cooked ham, cut into cubes
    1 pound sharp cheese, grated

1. Melt butter in vegetable pan; add flour; stir until smooth. Add hot milk, stirring constantly; cook over <u>medium</u>-<u>low</u> heat until thickened, smooth. Add salt, pepper. Pour cream sauce over macaroni.
2. Put alternate layers of creamed macaroni, ham, cheese in greased No. 802 pan. Sprinkle cheese over top.
3. Place one quart boiling water in bottom of No. 844 pan; adjust steamer ring; place pan on ring; cover; steam 15 minutes.
4. Twelve servings.

General Directions for Cooking Puddings

1. Place 1 quart water in No. 844 pan; bring to boil. If desired, add one tablespoon cream of tartar or vinegar to this water to prevent discoloration of utensil.
2. Mix pudding according to recipe. Pour into buttered No. 802 pan.
3. Place No. 807 ring in No. 844 pan.
4. Place No. 802 pan on ring; cover with No. 843 cover.
5. Place over <u>high</u> heat until steam first escapes beneath cover.
6. Reduce heat to <u>low</u>; cook required time. See recipe.
7. To cook on Controlled Heat unit see chart, page 13.
8. If desired, puddings may be steamed over a roast instead of water. Brown meat first; adjust ring and No. 802 pan containing pudding in No. 844 pan; cover. Control heat as for the roast.

STEAMED DATE AND NUT TORTE

 2 eggs
 ¾ cup sugar
 2 tablespoons milk
 2 teaspoons baking powder
 1½ tablespoons all purpose flour
 1 cup chopped nuts
 1 cup chopped dates
 ½ pint whipping cream
 1 tablespoon sugar
 ½ teaspoon vanilla

1. Beat eggs until thick.
2. Add sugar, milk; mix thoroughly.
3. Sift dry ingredients over dates, nuts; add to egg mixture.
4. Pour into well greased No. 802 pan.
5. Adjust No. 817 steamer plate over boiling water in No. 844 pan.
6. Place No. 802 pan on steamer plate; cover with No. 845 cover.
7. Steam over boiling water or a roast 1 hour.
8. Whip cream until stiff; add sugar, vanilla.
9. Top torte with whipped cream before serving.
10. Six servings.

ARABIAN NIGHT PUDDING

 1½ cups graham cracker crumbs (approximately 16 graham crackers)
 ¾ cup chopped pecans
 ½ pound pitted dates, chopped
 2 tablespoons all purpose flour
 1 teaspoon salt
 2 tablespoons sugar
 2 teaspoons baking powder
 1 egg, slightly beaten
 1 cup milk
 1 teaspoon vanilla

1. Put graham crackers through food press to make crumbs.
2. Chop pecans, pitted dates; combine with crumbs.
3. Sift dry ingredients together; add to first mixture; mix.
4. Beat egg slightly; add milk, vanilla. Add to dry mixture; beat well.
5. Pour into well greased No. 802 pan.
6. Adjust No. 817 steamer plate over boiling water in No. 844 pan.
7. Place No. 802 pan on steamer plate; cover with No. 845 cover.
8. Steam over boiling water or a roast 1 hour 15 minutes.
9. Serve hot with hard sauce or whipped cream.
10. Six servings.

PUMPKIN PUDDING

    1½ cups cooked pumpkin, riced
    ¾ cup sugar
    ¾ teaspoon cinnamon
    ¾ teaspoon ginger
    3 eggs, well beaten
    1½ cups milk, scalded
    ½ teaspoon vanilla
    ½ teaspoon salt

1. Mix all ingredients together.
2. Pour pumpkin mixture into greased No. 802 pan.
3. Adjust No. 807 steamer ring over boiling water in No. 844 pan; place No. 802 pan in ring. Be sure bottom of pan does not touch water; cover.
4. Place over medium heat until vapor first escapes from under cover. Reduce heat to low; steam 1 hour 10 minutes — 1 hour 15 minutes or until silver knife inserted into center comes out clean.
5. Chill; serve with whipped cream.
6. Eight servings.

SPICED PEACH PUDDING

    1½ cups sifted all purpose flour
    ¼ cup sugar
    ¼ teaspoon cinnamon
    ¼ teaspoon nutmeg
    2 teaspoons baking powder
    ½ teaspoon salt
    4 tablespoons shortening
    2 cups sliced peaches
    ¼ — ⅓ cup milk
    2 tablespoons butter
    ¼ cup sugar
    Juice of ½ lemon

1. Sift dry ingredients together.
2. Cut shortening into dry ingredients using fork or pastry blender.
3. Remove skins from peaches by covering with boiling water 2 minutes, then plunging into cold water.
4. Add ½ cup chopped peaches to flour mixture; enough milk to make a soft dough.
5. Melt butter in bottom of No. 802 pan; add sugar, lemon juice, remaining peaches.
6. Pour batter over peaches.
7. Adjust No. 817 steamer plate over boiling water in No. 844 pan.
8. Place No. 802 pan on steamer plate; cover with No. 845 cover.
9. Steam over boiling water or roast 1½ hours.
10. Serve hot with lemon sauce or whipped cream.
11. Eight servings.

ENGLISH PLUM PUDDING

    ½ pound stale bread crumbs
    1 cup scalded milk
    ½ cup sugar
    4 egg yolks, beaten
    ½ pound raisins, seeded, cut into pieces
    ¼ pound currants
    2 tablespoons flour
    ¼ pound figs, finely chopped
    2 ounces candied cherries
    2 ounces citron, finely chopped
    ½ cup walnuts, chopped
    ½ pound suet, cut fine
    1 teaspoon nutmeg
    ¾ teaspoon cinnamon
    ⅓ teaspoon cloves
    1½ teaspoons salt
    ⅓ teaspoon mace
    ¼ cup fruit juice
    4 egg whites

1. Soak bread in hot milk; cool.
2. Add sugar, beaten egg yolks.
3. Blend raisins, currants with 2 tablespoons flour. Add bread custard mixture; add figs, cherries, citron, walnuts.
4. Cream suet; add nutmeg, cinnamon, cloves, salt, mace. Combine with first mixture; blend thoroughly.
5. Add fruit juice; mix.
6. Beat egg whites until stiff; fold into pudding mixture.
7. Pour into well greased No. 802 pan or into any well greased mold.
8. Steam bake 6 hours in the No. 825 roaster according to directions for steam baking fruit cake, page 86.
9. Eight servings.

BAKED CUSTARD
    5 eggs
    6 tablespoons sugar
    1 teaspoon salt
    1½ teaspoons vanilla
    4 cups milk
    Nutmeg

1. Beat eggs slightly; add sugar, salt, vanilla; mix. Add milk; blend.
2. Put into No. 802 pan. Sprinkle top with nutmeg.
3. Adjust No. 817 steamer plate over boiling water in No. 844 pan.
4. Place custard on steamer plate; cover with No. 845 cover.
5. Steam over boiling water or roast 15-20 minutes. When a silver knife inserted into custard comes out clean, custard is done; chill.
6. Six servings.

SAUCES

HOT BUTTERSCOTCH SAUCE
    ½ cup butter
    1 cup brown sugar
    1 tablespoon flour
    ½ cup boiling water
    1 teaspoon vanilla

1. Cream butter, sugar, flour.
2. Add boiling water, vanilla; beat.
3. Serve hot over Steamed Date Pudding.
4. Six servings.

LEMON SAUCE
    ¾ cup sugar
    1½ tablespoons cornstarch
    ⅛ teaspoon salt
    1½ cups boiling water
    3 tablespoons butter
    3 tablespoons lemon juice
    ½ teaspoon grated lemon rind

1. Mix together sugar, cornstarch, salt in vegetable pan.
2. Add boiling water gradually, stirring constantly; boil 5 minutes.
3. Remove from heat; add butter, lemon juice, lemon rind; blend.
4. Serve hot over pudding.
5. Six servings.

CHOCOLATE SAUCE
    1 15-ounce can sweetened condensed milk
    3 ounces unsweetened chocolate
    6 tablespoons hot water

1. Combine milk, chocolate, hot water in vegetable pan.
2. Place over low heat; cook until thick, smooth, stirring constantly. If a thinner sauce is desired, add more hot water; stir until smooth.
3. Serve hot over Chocolate Brownies.
4. Eight servings.

RUM SAUCE
    2 eggs
    1 cup sugar
    1 cup whipping cream
    Rum flavoring

1. Beat eggs until stiff; add sugar slowly; continue beating until mixture loses its grain.
2. Whip cream until stiff; fold into egg mixture.
3. Add flavoring to taste.
4. Serve very cold over hot pudding.
5. Eight servings.

FOAMY SAUCE
    4 tablespoons butter
    1 cup sugar
    2 egg whites, unbeaten
    1 teaspoon vanilla
    ⅛ teaspoon almond extract or
    ⅛ teaspoon lemon extract

1. Cream butter; add sugar gradually; cream together until light.
2. Add egg whites one at a time; beat well after each addition.
3. Add extract.
4. Pour into No. 802 pan; place on ring; heat over hot water until frothy, stirring occasionally.
5. Serve over Plum Pudding.
6. Six servings.

meats, fowl and fish

818 Cover

918 Utility Pan

825 Combination Roaster

WEAR-EVER NEW METHOD UTENSILS FOR...

meats, fowl and fish

845 Cover

817 Steamer Plate

802 Inner Pan

807 Ring

844 Pan

843 Cover

940 Broiler Pan

938 Fry Pan and Cover

843
940

For small roasts of meat, fowl or fish. For broiling steaks, chops, fish fillets, bacon.

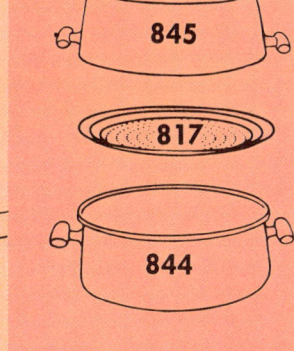

845
817
844

For medium sized roasts of meat, fowl or fish with steamed dried food or steamed potatoes.

845
802
817
844

For medium sized roasts of meat, fowl or fish with steamed dried food or pudding.

845
802
807
844

For baking meat loaf, chicken or oyster pot pie; ham with escalloped potatoes, etc.

WEAR-EVER

New Method Utensils can be used in many combinations, thus increasing their usefulness.

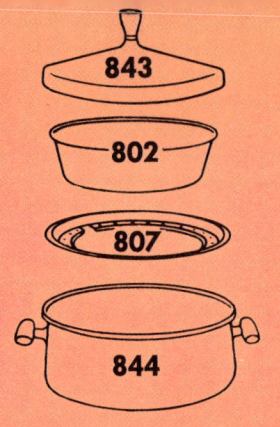

843
802
807
844

For medium sized roasts of meat, fowl or fish with steamed dried food or pudding.

818
918

For large steaks, large quantities of food; for large low roasts of meat, fowl or fish.

845
844

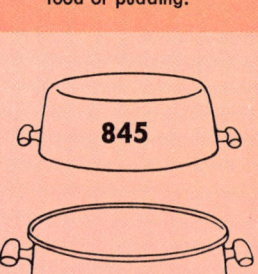

For medium sized high roasts of meat, fowl or fish.

843
844

For medium sized roasts of meat, fowl or fish. For soups or stews.

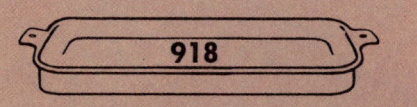

918

For broiling large quantities of steak, chops, fish fillets, bacon, sausage.

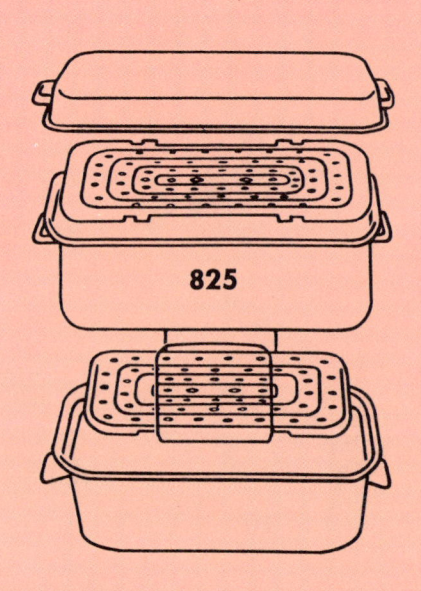

825

825

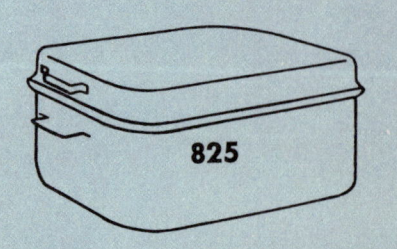

For large roasts of meat, fowl or fish.

For very large, high roasts of meat or fowl; for large low roasts of meat, fowl or fish with steamed dried food or pudding.

meats, fowl and fish

Directions for Top of Range Roasting

1. Place No. 844 pan over <u>high</u> heat. (Note explanation of <u>high</u> heat on pages 10, 15.)
2. Put a small piece of white paper (do not use tissue paper) in bottom; when this turns brown, pan is ready for use. Remove paper; place meat in pan.
3. Brown thoroughly on all sides, allowing about 10 minutes to a side. Meat will stick to hot pan at start, but will loosen itself when sufficiently browned. If meat does not stick to pan, it indicates pan was not hot enough and meat will not brown properly.
4. Reduce heat to <u>low</u>; cover pan with No. 843 cover if roast is small or No. 845 cover if roast is large.
5. New Method top of range roasting requires approximately the same length of time as oven roasting.
6. To roast on Controlled Heat unit see chart, page 13.
7. Seasoning may be added after browning, during or at end of cooking process.
8. Following the same procedure, small roasts may be roasted in No. 940 pan with No. 843 cover.

Directions for Pan Broiling

1. Heat No. 940 broiler pan over <u>high</u> heat. (Note explanation of <u>high</u> heat on pages 10, 15.)
2. Put a small piece of white paper (do not use tissue paper) in bottom; when this turns brown, pan is ready for use.
3. Remove paper; place meat in pan; brown on both sides.
4. Reduce heat to <u>medium</u>; cook meat to taste, turning several times; season.
5. To pan broil on Controlled Heat unit see chart, page 13.
6. If a large quantity of meat is to be pan broiled, use No. 918 pan.

Directions for Use of No. 825 Large Rectangular Roaster

1. Large roasts such as whole hams, large roasts of beef, large legs of lamb, turkey are roasted in the No. 825 rectangular roaster.
2. Place No. 825 bottom pan over high heat with control valve in the rear. (Note explanation of high heat on pages 10, 15.)
3. Put a small piece of white paper (do not use tissue paper) in bottom; when this turns brown, pan is ready for use.
4. Remove paper; add meat. Brown well on all sides, about 10 minutes to a side.
5. Remove meat from pan; adjust lifting rack; place meat on rack.
6. If roast is high, adjust No. 825 middle section, then cover with No. 825 cover with control valve to the front. Heat control valves in bottom section and cover must be at opposite ends of the roaster. If roast is small, the middle section is not necessary.
7. Adjust control valves according to directions given in recipe. In general, they are kept closed until roast is three-quarters done, then opened to allow for good browning.
8. Adjust heat under roaster according to directions given in recipe. If a "moderate" oven is desired, reduce heat to medium; if a "slow" oven is desired, reduce heat to low.
9. Allow about the same length of time as for oven roasting.
10. Salt or any other seasoning may be added after browning, during or at end of cooking process.
11. Do not use large roaster on controlled heat unit.

General Directions for Pan Broiling Chicken

1. Select fryer or roaster; cut into desired pieces; wash well.
2. Heat No. 940 pan or No. 844 pan and No. 845 cover over medium heat with ½ inch chicken fat.
3. Dip pieces into flour, crumbs or batter, or leave plain.
4. Put into hot fat; brown well on each side.
5. Reduce heat to low; cover; cook 35-45 minutes or until tender.

WARNING:—A cold pan placed over too intense heat or a hot pan into which cold water is poured may warp or buckle. To guard against this, heat the pan gradually. If it is necessary to pour water into a hot pan to make gravy, use warm water.

General Directions for Top of Range Roasting of Poultry

1. Singe, wash; clean and fully dress poultry.
2. Rub inside with salt.
3. Stuff poultry; do not pack dressing too tightly.
4. Skewer openings; lace with cord.
5. Twist tips of wings back and tuck under shoulders to hold wings close to body.
6. Tie legs together with cord; fasten to rump.
7. Dry poultry; spread breast, thighs, wings with shortening.
8. Heat No. 844 pan over <u>high</u> heat until a piece of white paper placed in bottom turns brown. (Note explanation of high heat on pages 10, 15.)
9. Reduce heat to <u>medium</u>; add poultry; brown well on all sides, turning frequently.
10. Turn breast side down.
11. Reduce heat to <u>low</u>; cover with No. 845 cover; roast 20-30 minutes per pound. Turn occasionally during roasting.
12. Season after poultry is browned.

MEATS

ROAST BEEF

    3½ pound roast (chuck, shoulder, tenderloin tip or rib)
    Salt, pepper, paprika

1. Heat No. 844 pan over <u>high</u> heat until a piece of white paper placed in bottom turns brown.
2. Reduce heat to <u>medium</u>; add roast; brown well on all sides—about 20 minutes.
3. Reduce heat to <u>low</u>; cover with No. 843 cover or No. 845 cover; roast 15 minutes per pound for rare; 25 minutes per pound for medium; 35 minutes per pound for well done.
4. Season near end of cooking time with salt, pepper, paprika.
5. Steamed onions (cooked whole over meat) centers removed and cavities filled with peas and carrots form an attractive garnish.
6. Eight servings.

MEAT LOAF

    2½ pounds beef, ground
    ½ pound smoked ham, ground
    ½ cup chopped onions
    2 tablespoons prepared mustard
    1 cup cracker crumbs
    1 tablespoon salt
    ½ teaspoon baking powder
    2 eggs, well beaten
    1¼ cups milk

1. Place all ingredients in mixing bowl blend thoroughly.
2. Shape into loaf.
3. This meat may be baked in No. 940 pan with No. 843 cover or No. 844 pan with No. 843 cover. Bake over <u>low</u> heat 1 hour 10 minutes.
4. When done, loosen meat loaf from pan with spatula; lift from pan; place on platter; garnish.
5. Eight to ten servings.

SWISS STEAK

   Salt, pepper
   1/2 cup flour
   2 pounds round steak (cut 2 1/2 inches thick)
   2 tablespoons fat
   1 medium sized onion
   1/2 green pepper, chopped fine
   1 cup tomatoes, strained

1. Mix salt, pepper, flour; pound into meat.
2. Melt fat in No. 844 pan over medium heat; add meat; brown well on each side.
3. Add onion, green pepper, tomatoes.
4. Reduce heat to low; cover with No. 845 cover; cook 2 hours.
5. For gravy, thicken juices in pan.
6. Eight servings.

HAMBURGER STEAK

   1 pound beef, ground
   1 large green pepper, chopped
   2 small onions, chopped
   Salt

1. Mix all together; form into flat cakes.
2. Heat No. 940 pan over high heat until a piece of white paper placed in bottom turns brown.
3. Reduce heat to medium; add meat; brown well on both sides, turning frequently.
4. Four servings.

LIVER

1. Place No. 940 pan over medium heat.
2. Melt 2 tablespoons fat in pan.
3. Add sliced liver; brown well on both sides, turning frequently.
4. Season with salt, pepper.
5. If desired, sliced onions may be cooked along with the liver.

CORNED BEEF AND CABBAGE

1. Soak 2 pounds corned beef overnight in cold water, or place 3 cups cold water, meat in No. 844 pan; cover with No. 845 cover; allow to cook over low heat 30 minutes.
2. Drain meat thoroughly; pour off water; dry pan.
3. Heat No. 844 pan over high heat until a piece of white paper placed in bottom turns brown.
4. Reduce heat to medium; add meat; brown on all sides.
5. Reduce heat to low; cover; cook 30 minutes.
6. Place 1 pound cabbage wedges in bottom of pan; put corned beef on top; cover with second pound of wedges.
7. Cover with No. 845 cover; cook 45-55 minutes.
8. Eight servings.

PAN BROILED STEAK

1. Trim excess fat, bone from steak.
2. Heat No. 940 pan over high heat until a piece of white paper placed in bottom turns brown.
3. Reduce heat to medium; add meat; brown well on both sides.
4. Turn frequently; continue to cook to desired degree of doneness.
5. Season; serve.

PORK CHOPS

1. Trim excess fat from chops.
2. Heat No. 940 pan over high heat until a piece of white paper placed in bottom turns brown.
3. Reduce heat to medium; add meat; brown well on both sides; cover.
4. Reduce heat to low; cook 35-45 minutes or until tender.
5. Season; serve.

STUFFED SPARE RIBS

    2 pounds spare ribs
  1½ cups bread cubes
    1 medium onion, minced
    2 tablespoons chopped parsley
    1 tablespoon melted butter
    ½ teaspoon salt
    ⅛ teaspoon pepper
    1 tablespoon water

1. Wipe meat; sprinkle with salt.
2. Mix bread, onion, parsley, melted butter, seasonings, water together.
3. Spread over spare ribs; roll; fasten with skewers; tie with string.
4. Heat No. 844 pan over high heat until a piece of white paper placed in bottom turns brown.
5. Reduce heat to medium; add meat; brown well on all sides.
6. Reduce heat to low; cover with No. 845 cover; cook 1½ hours.
7. Four servings.

SAUSAGE

1. Prick skins to prevent bursting.
2. Heat No. 940 pan over high heat until a piece of white paper placed in bottom turns brown.
3. Reduce heat to medium; add meat; brown well on all sides; cover.
4. Reduce heat to low; cook 15-20 minutes or until tender.
5. Serve at once.

ROAST LOIN OF PORK

1. Wipe 3 pounds loin of pork.
2. Heat No. 844 pan over high heat until a piece of white paper placed in bottom turns brown.
3. Reduce heat to medium; add meat; brown well on all sides.
4. Turn fat side up; season.
5. Roast over low heat; cover with No. 845 cover; allow 30-35 minutes per pound.
6. Six servings.

SAUERKRAUT AND PORK

1. Have bone broken in center of 4 pound loin roast. Cut into two parts for No. 844 pan.
2. Heat No. 844 pan over high heat until a piece of white paper placed in bottom turns brown.
3. Reduce heat to medium; add meat; brown well on all sides.
4. Reduce heat to low; cover with No. 845 cover; cook 2 hours.

SAUERKRAUT

1. Peel, dice 1 small onion.
2. Mix with 2 pounds sauerkraut.
3. Place in No. 802 pan on No. 817 steamer plate over pork roast.
4. Cook 1 hour 15 minutes.
5. Eight servings.

PORK TURKEYS

    8 double loin pork chops (cut about ¾ inch thick)
  2¾ cups bread cubes
    5 tablespoons butter, melted
    1 small onion, minced
    ½ teaspoon Worcestershire sauce
    ½ teaspoon salt
    ⅛ teaspoon pepper
    5 tablespoons ketchup

1. Have butcher cut pocket in each chop.
2. Make dressing of bread, butter, onion, seasonings. Do not put ketchup in dressing. Place dressing in pocket of each chop. Close openings.
3. Heat No. 844 pan and No. 845 cover over high heat until a piece of white paper placed in bottom turns brown.
4. Reduce heat to medium; add meat; brown well on both sides in each pan at the same time.
5. Place chops in No. 844 pan; pour ketchup over top.
6. Reduce heat to low; cover with No. 845 cover; cook 1 hour.
7. Eight servings.

BAKED HAM

    4 pounds ham, butt end
    4 tablespoons brown sugar
    10 whole cloves

1. Wipe ham with damp cloth; remove brown spots caused by curing.
2. Heat No. 844 pan over high heat until a piece of white paper placed in bottom turns brown.
3. Reduce heat to medium; add meat; brown on all sides; turn fat side up.
4. Reduce heat to low; cover with No. 845 cover; cook 30 minutes.
5. Score fat side with diagonal cuts to form diamonds; insert a clove in center of each diamond; pat brown sugar over surface.
6. Cover; cook 30 minutes longer.
7. Six servings.

HAM AND PINEAPPLE

    1½ pounds ham
    1 No. 2 can pineapple, crushed or sliced
    1 tablespoon brown sugar
    7 whole cloves

1. Ham should be cut 1 inch thick.
2. Heat No. 940 pan over high heat until a piece of white paper placed in bottom turns brown.
3. Reduce heat to medium; add meat; brown well on each side.
4. Drain pineapple; pour 1 cup juice over ham.
5. Sprinkle with sugar; insert cloves; place pineapple on ham.
6. Reduce heat to low; cover with No. 843 cover; cook 30-40 minutes.
7. Six servings.

PAN BROILED HAM

1. Trim excess fat from ham slice.
2. Heat No. 940 pan over high heat until a piece of white paper placed in bottom turns brown.
3. Reduce heat to medium; add meat; brown well on both sides.
4. Turn frequently; continue to cook until done.

PAN BROILED BACON

1. Place bacon in cold No. 940 pan.
2. Place over low heat.
3. Turn frequently; drain off excess fat during browning.
4. Cook until crisp; drain on paper.

PINEAPPLE HAM LOAF

    1¼ pounds cured ham, ground
    ¾ pound lean fresh pork, ground
    1 cup cracker crumbs
    2 eggs, beaten slightly
    ¾ cup milk
    2 tablespoons mustard
    3 tablespoons brown sugar
    6 pineapple slices, well drained
    6 maraschino cherries

1. Mix well all ingredients except brown sugar, pineapple, cherries.
2. Sprinkle brown sugar in No. 940 pan; arrange pineapple rings; place a cherry in center of each ring.
3. Pat ham loaf mixture over entire surface of pineapple. This just fills No. 940 pan.
4. Cover with No. 843 cover.
5. Place over medium heat until cover becomes hot to touch.
6. Reduce heat to low; cook 1 hour.
7. When done, tilt cover, drain off all excess liquid in bottom of pan.
8. Remove cover; place meat platter over meat loaf; invert pan.
9. Eight servings.

SWEETBREADS

1. Combine ¼ cup flour, ½ teaspoon salt, ⅛ teaspoon pepper in clean paper bag.
2. Wash sweetbreads; trim; drop into bag; shake to coat with flour.
3. Melt 3 tablespoons butter in No. 940 pan over medium heat; add sweetbreads; brown on both sides; cover.
4. Reduce heat to low; cook 10 minutes.

VEAL BALLS PAPRIKA

    ¾ pound veal, ground
    ¼ pound pork, ground
    ½ cup minced onion
  1½ teaspoons salt
    ⅛ teaspoon pepper
    ½ cup dry bread crumbs
    ½ cup milk
    1 egg, beaten
    3 tablespoons butter
    ½ teaspoon paprika
    ¾ cup diced celery
    ¼ cup water

1. Combine veal, pork, 3 tablespoons onion, salt, pepper, bread crumbs, milk, egg; form into 18 balls.
2. Melt 1 tablespoon butter in No. 940 pan over medium heat; add meat balls; brown on all sides; sprinkle with paprika.
3. Brown remainder of onion in 2 tablespoons butter; add celery, water; cover; cook 10 minutes.
4. Pour onion, celery mixture over meat balls; cover.
5. Reduce heat to low; cook 20 minutes.
6. Dissolve 2 tablespoons flour, ½ teaspoon salt in ½ cup cream; pour over meat; blend with juice in pan.
7. Cover; cook 15 minutes longer.
8. Four servings.

VEAL STEAK

1. Heat No. 940 pan over high heat until a piece of white paper placed in bottom turns brown.
2. Reduce heat to medium; add meat; brown well on both sides; cover.
3. Reduce heat to low; cook 20-25 minutes or until tender.
4. Season; serve.

VEAL CHOPS

1. Heat No. 940 pan over high heat until a piece of white paper placed in bottom turns brown.
2. Reduce heat to medium; add meat; brown well on both sides; cover.
3. Reduce heat to low; cook 20-25 minutes or until tender.
4. Season; serve.

BRAISED STUFFED BREAST OF VEAL

  3½ pounds breast of veal with pocket
    2 cups fine bread crumbs
    1 small onion, minced
    ½ cup diced celery
    2 tablespoons butter
    ¼ cup water
    ¼ cup grated cheese
    1 teaspoon salt
    ⅛ teaspoon pepper

1. Wipe meat with damp cloth.
2. Mix all ingredients well.
3. Fill pocket; skewer; lace with cord.
4. Heat No. 844 pan over high heat until a piece of white paper placed in bottom turns brown.
5. Reduce heat to medium; add meat; brown well on all sides.
6. Reduce heat to low; cover with No. 845 cover; cook 2 hours.
7. Six servings.

VEAL AND HAM LOAF

    1½ pounds veal shoulder, ground
    1½ pounds cured ham, ground
    ½ cup cracker crumbs
    1 teaspoon salt
    ¼ teaspoon pepper
    ¼ cup minced onion
    2 teaspoons Worcestershire sauce
    1½ cups milk

1. Mix all ingredients well.
2. Mold meat mixture into loaf; place in No. 940 pan.
3. Cover with No. 843 cover.
4. Place over <u>medium</u> heat until cover is hot to touch.
5. Reduce heat to <u>low</u>; cook 1½ hours.
6. When one-half the cooking time has elapsed, remove cover; turn meat loaf. This browns each side.
7. Eight servings.

ROAST LEG OF LAMB

1. Have butcher cut off bone at first joint; french; skewer; wipe.
2. Remove fell; rub with garlic.
3. Heat No. 844 pan over <u>high</u> heat until a piece of white paper placed in bottom turns brown.
4. Reduce heat to <u>medium</u>; add meat; brown well on all sides.
5. Reduce heat to <u>low</u>; cover with No. 845 cover; cook 30-35 minutes per pound.
6. Season with salt, pepper near end of cooking time.
7. Serve with mint sauce.
8. Eight servings.

BROILED LAMB CHOPS

1. Remove excess fat from chops.
2. Heat No. 940 pan over <u>high</u> heat until a piece of white paper placed in bottom turns brown.
3. Reduce heat to <u>medium</u>; add meat; brown well on both sides.
4. Turn frequently; continue to cook until done.
5. Season; serve.

IRISH STEW WITH DUMPLINGS

    3 pounds lamb shoulder (cut into small pieces)
    ¾ cup cooked carrots
    ½ cup cooked turnips
    4 cups cooked potatoes

1. Heat No. 844 pan over <u>high</u> heat until a piece of white paper placed in bottom turns brown.
2. Reduce heat to <u>medium</u>; add meat; brown well on all sides.
3. Add water to cover; bring to boil; reduce heat to <u>low</u>. Cover; cook 2 hours. (Water is necessary to extract the juices from the meat and not for cooking.)
4. Twenty minutes before serving add vegetables, sufficient water to make 3 cups liquid. Season with salt.
5. Prepare dumplings, page 92; drop on stew; cover; cook 10 minutes.
6. Cover should not be removed until dumplings are ready to serve.
7. Eight servings.

LAMB CURRY

    2 tablespoons butter
    ¾ cup sliced onions
    1 cup diced celery
    1 minced clove garlic
    1½ cups cubed cooked lamb
    1 teaspoon curry powder
    2 cups stock or lamb gravy
    Salt
    2 tablespoons flour
    ¼ cup cold water

1. Melt butter in No. 940 pan; sauté onion, celery, garlic in butter until lightly browned.
2. Add lamb, curry powder, stock, salt; cover with No. 843 cover; simmer over <u>low</u> heat 30 minutes.
3. Make paste from flour, water; stir into curry to thicken; simmer 5 minutes uncovered.
4. Serve over fluffy rice.
5. Four servings.

FOWL
FRIED CHICKEN

1. Select fryer or roaster; cut into desired pieces; wash well.
2. Heat No. 844 pan, No. 845 cover over medium heat; add ½ cup chicken fat.
3. Dip pieces into flour, crumbs or batter or leave plain.
4. To flour or crumb: put flour or fine cracker crumbs, seasonings into clean paper bag. Drop pieces of chicken into bag; close opening; shake until chicken is coated.
5. Put into hot fat; brown well on each side; season.
6. If further cooking of chicken is required to make it tender, place in No. 844 pan; cover with No. 845 cover.
7. Reduce heat to low; cook 35-40 minutes or until tender.

CHICKEN MARYLAND

  2 young chickens
 1½ teaspoons salt
  ½ teaspoon pepper
 1½ cups dry crumbs
  1 egg, well beaten
  ½ cup shortening
  3 tablespoons flour
  1 teaspoon salt
  ¼ teaspoon pepper
 1½ cups milk

1. Singe; clean; cut up chickens.
2. Mix seasonings, crumbs; beat egg.
3. Dip into beaten egg; roll in seasoned crumbs.
4. Melt shortening in No. 844 pan; heat over medium heat; add chicken.
5. Cover with No. 845 cover.
6. Reduce heat to low; cook approximately 45 minutes. Turn occasionally to insure even browning.
7. Remove chicken; make gravy by adding flour, salt, pepper, milk to pan.
8. Strain gravy through food press; serve over rice.
9. Eight servings.

NEW METHOD FRIED CHICKEN

Select fryer or roaster. Have butcher cut into desired pieces. Small fryers are best halved for individual servings; wash chicken.

Without Added Grease:

1. Place chicken in cold No. 940 broiler pan; cover.
2. Place over medium heat until cover becomes hot to touch; reduce to low.
3. Cook 50 minutes. Remove cover; turn heat to high.
4. Turn pieces of chicken frequently to insure even browning. If large quantity of chicken is to be fried, add about ½ cup water while frying to give more liquor.

With Added Grease:

1. Heat No. 844 pan and No. 845 cover over medium-high heat. Add 3 tablespoons butter or chicken fat to each pan.
2. Dry chicken; put into hot fat. When chicken starts to brown, reduce heat to medium; turn pieces until an even brown.
3. If further cooking of chicken is required to make it tender, place all of chicken in No. 844 pan; cover; reduce heat to low; cook ½ hour or until tender.
4. If desired, chicken can be floured before frying. To flour: put flour, seasonings into clean, strong paper bag. Drop pieces of chicken into bag; close opening; shake until chicken is evenly, lightly floured.

CHICKEN ALMOND

    3 tablespoons butter
    ¾ cup celery, cut into 1 inch pieces
    ¼ cup sliced onion
    2 cups diced cooked chicken
    ½ cup canned mushrooms
    1 tablespoon cornstarch
    3 tablespoons soy sauce
    1 cup clear chicken consommé
    1 cup unsalted toasted almonds

1. Melt butter in No. 940 pan; add celery, onion.
2. Stir; cook 2 minutes or until soft.
3. Add chicken, mushrooms; cook over low heat about 10 minutes.
4. Combine corn starch, soy sauce, consommé; stir slowly into chicken mixture; heat to boiling point.
5. Stir in almonds.
6. Serve on hot fluffy rice.
7. Six servings.

ROAST STUFFED CHICKEN

1. Singe; clean; dress 4 pound roasting chicken.
2. Rub with salt inside and out.
3. Stuff chicken; do not pack too tightly.
4. Skewer openings; lace with cord.
5. Twist tip of wings back and tuck under shoulders to hold wings close to body of bird.
6. Tie legs together with cord; fasten to rump.
7. Dry chicken; spread breast, thighs, wings with melted shortening.
8. Heat No. 844 pan over high heat until a piece of white paper placed in bottom turns brown.
9. Reduce heat to medium; put bird into pan; brown well on all sides.
10. Turn breast side down.
11. Reduce heat to low; cover with No. 845 cover; roast 25-30 minutes per pound.
12. Turn occasionally during roasting period to insure even browning.

ROAST TURKEY

1. Singe; clean; dress turkey. Rub inside with salt.
2. Stuff turkey; do not pack too tightly.
3. Skewer openings; lace with cord.
4. Twist tips of wings back and tuck under shoulders to hold wings close to body of bird.
5. Tie legs together with cord; fasten to rump.
6. Dry turkey; brush with melted butter; sprinkle with salt, pepper.
7. Heat No. 825 roaster over high heat until a piece of white paper placed in bottom turns brown.
8. Reduce heat to medium; add lifting rack.
9. Place bird on its side on rack; adjust middle section and place cover.
10. Heat control valves in bottom section and cover should be at opposite ends. Close valves; open for last hour of roasting time.
11. Roast 20-25 minutes per pound. Turn bird every hour.

TURKEY DEVONSHIRE

1. Heat 1 can cream of mushroom soup; thin with ½ cup cream; add 1 cup grated Cheddar cheese; stir until cheese is melted.
2. Arrange sliced white meat of turkey on white toast; top with slice of baked ham, mushroom sauce.
3. Place under broiler until sauce bubbles and browns slightly.

CHICKEN TERRAPIN

- ½ cup butter
- 1 cup flour
- 1 tablespoon salt
- ⅛ teaspoon pepper
- ⅛ teaspoon paprika
- 3½ cups milk
- 2½ cups chicken broth
- 1 No. 2 can mushrooms (2 cups)
- 2 hard cooked eggs (cut into cubes)
- 1 No. 2 can small peas
- 1 can pimento (4 pods) cut into strips
- 4 cups cooked, diced chicken (meat from 3½ lb. fowl)
- 1 tablespoon lemon juice

1. Melt butter in vegetable pan. Add flour, seasonings; stir until well blended.
2. Add milk, chicken broth; cook until slightly thickened, stirring constantly.
3. Add mushrooms, eggs, peas, pimentos; cook a few minutes.
4. Add chicken carefully.
5. Keep warm in No. 802 pan on ring over hot water in No. 844 pan.
6. Just before serving, add lemon juice.
7. Serve over toast.
8. Sixteen servings.

CHICKEN IN CASSEROLE

- 1 4 pound chicken
- 2 teaspoons salt
- 2 stalks celery
- 2 cups water
- 18 peeled white onions
- ⅓ cup butter
- ⅓ cup flour
- ⅔ teaspoon salt
- ¼ teaspoon mace
- 1¾ cups chicken stock
- 1 cup top milk
- ¾ teaspoon tarragon
- ½ cup corn flakes

1. Place chicken, salt, celery, water in No. 844 pan; cover.
2. Cook over low heat 1½ hours. Add onions last half hour of cooking time.
3. Bone chicken; arrange with onions in No. 802 pan. Cover with sauce.

To Make Sauce:
1. Melt butter; add flour, salt, mace. Stir until smooth; add chicken stock, milk. Cook until thickened; add tarragon.
2. Adjust steamer ring over boiling water in No. 844 pan; place No. 802 pan on ring; cover; steam 45 minutes.
3. Sprinkle with crushed corn flakes before serving.
4. Eight servings.

CHICKEN AND NOODLE SCALLOP

- 1 cup or 8 ounce package broad noodles
- 2 cups boiling water
- 2 tablespoons shortening
- 2 tablespoons chopped green pepper
- 1 teaspoon minced onion
- 1½ cups cooked chicken
- Bread crumbs
- 2 cups white sauce
- ½ cup grated cheese

1. Place noodles in No. 802 pan. Add boiling water; place pan on ring over boiling water in No. 844 pan.
2. Cover; steam over medium heat ½ hour or until noodles are tender.
3. Drain; rinse noodles.
4. Melt shortening in No. 940 pan; add green pepper, onion; cook over low heat 5 minutes.
5. Add onion, green pepper mixture to chicken; combine with white sauce; stir in noodles.
6. Pour chicken-noodle mixture into buttered No. 802 pan; sprinkle with grated cheese.
7. Adjust steamer ring over boiling water in No. 844 pan; place No. 802 pan on ring; cover; steam over low heat 20-25 minutes.
8. Sprinkle with crumbs just before serving.
9. Eight servings.

ROAST LONG ISLAND DUCK

Select 3½-4½ pound duck drawn weight.

1. If duck is not drawn, draw; remove head, feet.
2. Singe; clean; wash; dry duck.
3. Fill cavity with quartered apples, two large quartered onions, several stalks of celery to give flavor but remove before serving.
4. Truss bird or not as needed; sometimes legs and wings are too short to truss.
5. Heat No. 825 roaster over high heat until a piece of white paper placed in bottom turns brown.
6. Reduce heat to medium; brown duck on all sides.
7. Remove duck; adjust lifting rack; place duck on back on rack; pierce skin in several places to let fat escape.
8. Season with salt and pepper; cover.
9. Heat control valves in bottom section and cover should be at opposite ends. Close valves; open during last hour of roasting time.
10. Roast 30 minutes per pound.
11. Serve on hot platter with Orange Sauce.
12. Four servings.

FISH

TO POACH FISH

1. Put 2 cups boiling water into No. 940 pan; add 1½ teaspoons salt, 1 slice lemon, 1 slice onion, 2 sprigs parsley, ¼ teaspoon pepper, 1 bay leaf; boil 5 minutes.
2. Reduce heat to low; add fish; cover; simmer gently 10 minutes or until fish flakes easily with a fork. If fish is thick, turn once during cooking.

BROILED FISH

1. Scale; split; clean fish; wipe dry.
2. Melt 2 tablespoons shortening in No. 940 pan over medium heat.
3. Place fish in pan; skin side up.
4. Reduce heat to medium-low.
5. Broil 15-20 minutes or until golden brown and tender.
6. This method is used for all small whole fish such as bass, pickerel, blue fish, red snapper, white fish, trout and mackerel.

SALTED FISH

1. Place fish flesh side down in pan.
2. Cover with cold water; soak 48 hours.
3. Drain; add fresh water to cover.
4. Cover; bring to boil; simmer 20 minutes or until tender.
5. Drain; serve with Tomato Sauce.

SOUTHERN STYLE PERCH

Part 1
12 fillets of perch
2 eggs, well beaten
3 tablespoons flour
5 tablespoons shortening
Salt, pepper, paprika

Part 2
½ cup tomato paste
½ cup milk
1 teaspoon cornstarch

1. Dip fish into egg; roll in flour.
2. Melt shortening in No. 940 pan over medium heat.
3. Brown six fillets at a time.
4. After all are browned, place together; season with salt, pepper, paprika.
5. Reduce heat to low; cover; cook 20 minutes.
6. Remove fillets to platter.
7. Combine tomato paste, milk, cornstarch; add to drippings in pan.
8. Bring to boil; pour over fish.
9. Six servings.

STEAMED FISH

1. Sprinkle fish with salt; place on No. 817 steamer plate.
2. Steam covered over boiling water until tender or until meat can be readily flaked with a fork.
3. Fish with a dry meat such as cod, haddock, halibut, salmon are best for steaming.
4. Steamed fish may be served hot with sauce or chilled and flaked for use in salads.

BAKED STUFFED FISH

    1 2½ pound fish or
    2 fish steaks, such as halibut, salmon or swordfish
Stuffing:
  1½ cups bread, cubed
   ½ teaspoon salt
   1 small onion, minced
   ¼ cup celery
   1 tablespoon lemon juice
   ⅓ cup melted butter
   1 tablespoon parsley, cut fine
   Water to hold together if moist stuffing is desired

1. Clean fish; bone; remove head, tail.
2. Dry; sprinkle inside with salt.
3. Mix ingredients for stuffing in order given; pack lightly into fish.
4. Sew up opening; rub outside of fish with butter or cooking oil.
5. Place a piece of Alcoa Wrap aluminum foil in No. 825 roaster covering two sides as far as cover. Melt one tablespoon butter on foil; place stuffed fish in roaster.
6. Cover; bake over <u>medium</u>-<u>low</u> heat one hour.
7. Remove to platter.
8. Serve with Yukon Sauce; garnish with lemon, parsley.
9. If steaks are used, arrange stuffing on one steak, place second steak over stuffing. Insert toothpicks through both steaks, one inch apart; lace firmly with cord.
10. Six servings.

BAKED FISH CREOLE

   3 pounds perch fillet
   ¼ teaspoon salt
   ⅛ teaspoon pepper
   3 tablespoons butter
   2 tablespoons flour
   ½ cup sliced mushrooms
   6 tomatoes, quartered
   1 large onion, sliced
   1 bay leaf
   1 teaspoon thyme
   1 cup white wine
   ½ cup cracker crumbs
   2 sprigs parsley

1. Clean; wash fish; season with salt, pepper.
2. Melt butter in No. 940 pan; add flour; brown lightly; add mushrooms, tomatoes, onion; simmer 10 minutes.
3. Place fish in No. 918 pan; pour butter-flour mixture over fish; sprinkle with herbs; pour wine over all; bake uncovered over <u>low</u> heat 20 minutes; sprinkle with buttered crumbs.
4. Garnish with parsley.
5. Six servings.

SALMON LOAF

   2 cups canned salmon
   1 cup soft bread crumbs
   3 eggs
   2 teaspoons lemon juice
   ½ teaspoon salt
   ¼ cup melted butter
   ¼ cup liquid from salmon
   1 teaspoon chopped parsley
   lemon wedges

1. Remove bones, black skin from salmon; flake with a fork. Do not mash.
2. Add bread crumbs, beaten eggs, seasonings, butter, liquid from salmon.
3. Mix thoroughly. Turn into greased No. 844 pan. Shape into loaf.
4. Cover; cook over <u>low</u> heat one hour.
5. Serve with hot white sauce; garnish with parsley, lemon.
6. Six servings.

SHRIMP FLOUNDER ROLLS

    6 flounder fillets
    Salt, pepper
    1 tablespoon mayonnaise
    1 teaspoon prepared mustard
    2 tablespoons softened butter
    2 tablespoons minced parsley
    1 pound shrimp, cooked, shelled, cleaned
    2 cups canned tomatoes
    2/3 cup soft bread crumbs
    6 tablespoons butter, melted

1. Cut each fillet in half lengthwise; rub with salt, pepper.
2. Blend together mayonnaise, mustard, butter, parsley; spread mixture over fillets.
3. Place 2 shrimp in each fillet; roll like jelly roll with shrimp inside; fasten with toothpicks.
4. Melt 2 tablespoons shortening in No. 940 pan over medium heat; add rolls, remaining shrimp.
5. Pour tomatoes over all.
6. Brown bread crumbs in melted butter; sprinkle over top; cover.
7. Reduce heat to low; cook 25 minutes.
8. Six servings.

CREOLE SHRIMP

    4 tablespoons butter
    2 green onions, chopped
    1/2 green pepper, chopped
    1 cup celery, chopped
    1/4 teaspoon crushed sage
    1 teaspoon salt
    1/4 teaspoon Tabasco sauce
    1 cup tomato juice
    2 cups cleaned green shrimp
    2 cups steamed rice

1. Melt butter in No. 940 pan; brown onion, pepper, celery lightly.
2. Add sage, salt, Tabasco sauce, tomato juice; bring to boil.
3. Add shrimp; simmer uncovered 30 minutes.
4. Serve over steamed rice.
5. Four servings.

TO COOK FRESH SHRIMP

1. Place 1 quart water, a slice of lemon in bottom of No. 844 pan. Adjust No. 817 steamer plate; cover with No. 845 cover. Place over high heat until water comes to rapid boil.
2. Wash shrimp in cold water; place on steamer plate; cover. Reduce heat to medium; steam 15 minutes.
3. Remove shells. With paring knife cut around circumference deep enough to expose black thread which is the intestine. Remove all of intestine.

LOBSTER CARDINAL IN PATTY SHELL

    3 whole live lobsters or 3 pounds lobster tails
    12 tablespoons butter
    12 tablespoons flour
    1 1/2 teaspoons salt
    3 cups milk

1. Bring water to rolling boil in No. 825 roaster; add 1 teaspoon salt per quart water.
2. Plunge live lobster, head first, into boiling water.
3. Allow water to come to boil before adding each lobster.
4. After water returns to boil, cook 20 minutes.
5. Remove lobster from water; drain.
6. Split down through center; remove intestinal vein, stomach. Remove coral; mash; remove meat; dice.
7. Crack claws; remove meat; dice.
8. Melt butter; add flour, seasoning.
9. Stir until well blended. Add milk gradually, stirring constantly.
10. Bring to boil; cook 2 minutes.
11. Stir in mashed coral; add lobster.
12. Serve in patty shells; garnish with water cress.
13. Lobster tails may be used. Cook in salted boiling water 15 minutes. Remove from shell; dice.
14. Vegetable coloring may be used in cream sauce to give added color.
15. Six servings.

OYSTERS

    1 pint oysters
    Seasoned bread crumbs
    2 tablespoons butter

1. Clean oysters; sprinkle both sides with salt.
2. Take up by tough muscle with silver fork; dip into crumbs.
3. Melt butter in No. 940 pan over medium heat; add oysters; brown on both sides.
4. Serve at once.
5. Four servings.

OYSTER AND FILLET OF SOLE ROLLS

    1 pound fillet of sole
    1 pint Select oysters
    2 tablespoons butter
    Juice, 1/2 lemon
    Salt
    2 tablespoons butter
    2 tablespoons flour
    1/4 teaspoon salt
    1/4 teaspoon pepper
    1/8 teaspoon tarragon
    1 cup milk

1. Cut fillet of sole into strips 1 inch x 3 inches.
2. Drain oysters.
3. Wrap each oyster in strip of sole; pin with toothpick.
4. Saute in melted butter in No. 940 pan; sprinkle with lemon juice, salt.
5. Make white sauce by melting butter in saucepan; stir in flour, salt, pepper, tarragon to make smooth paste; add milk; stir until thickened.
6. Place oyster-sole rolls in No. 802 pan; remove toothpicks; add white sauce.
7. Place on ring over hot water in No. 844 pan; cover; steam 15-20 minutes; sprinkle with buttered crumbs.
8. Four servings.

OYSTER POT PIE

    4 tablespoons butter
    1/2 cup minced onion
    4 tablespoons flour
    Oyster liquor with enough milk to make 2 cups
    1 1/2 cups mushrooms, sliced thin
    3 tablespoons chopped parsley
    1 quart small oysters
    Salt
    Pepper
    Savory biscuit dough
    Paprika

1. Melt butter in No. 802 pan over low heat; add onion; cook until soft and yellow.
2. Add flour; blend well; add milk and oyster liquid gradually; stir until smooth.
3. Add mushrooms, parsley, oysters, salt, pepper.
4. Adjust No. 807 ring in No. 844 pan; place No. 802 pan on ring; cover with No. 845 cover; heat over high heat 10 minutes.
5. Make Savory biscuit dough; pat to 3/8 inch thickness; cut with one inch cutter. Arrange biscuits on top of creamed oysters. Sprinkle paprika over biscuits.
6. Bake over high heat 10 minutes; reduce heat to medium; bake 15 minutes or until biscuits are done.

OYSTER STEW

1. Melt 1/4 cup butter in No. 940 pan; add 1/4 teaspoon grated onion, 24 drained oysters; heat only until edges of oysters curl slightly.
2. Add 1 pint milk, 1 pint cream, 3/4 teaspoon salt, 1/8 teaspoon pepper; heat over high heat but do not boil.
3. Serve with dash of paprika, lump of butter.
4. Four servings.

EGGS—CHEESE

SCRAMBLED EGGS

    2 tablespoons shortening
    8 eggs
    ¾ teaspoon salt
    ⅛ teaspoon pepper
    ¾ cup milk

1. Melt shortening or butter in No. 802 pan over low heat.
2. Beat eggs slightly; add remaining ingredients; beat thoroughly.
3. Pour into No. 802 pan.
4. Adjust No. 807 ring over boiling water in No. 844 pan.
5. Place No. 802 pan on ring; cook until thick and creamy; occasionally scraping from sides and bottom.
6. If you prefer, melt shortening in No. 940 pan; add egg mixture; cook over low heat, stirring constantly.
7. Four servings.

OMELET

    4 eggs
    4 tablespoons hot water
    ¾ teaspoon salt
    ⅛ teaspoon pepper
    1 tablespoon butter, melted

1. Beat egg whites until stiff. Beat yolks until thick and lemon colored; beat in hot water; add salt, pepper.
2. Fold egg whites into yolks.
3. Butter bottom and side of No. 940 pan; heat over low heat 5 minutes.
4. Pour egg mixture into pan. Cook uncovered until top is firm to the touch.
5. Fold in half; turn onto platter; serve at once.
6. If desired, ¾ cup diced cooked meat, ⅓ cup grated American cheese, 1 cup cooked vegetables or ½ cup tomato sauce may be spread over top before folding.
7. Two servings.

FRIED EGGS

1. Melt 1 tablespoon shortening in No. 940 pan over low heat.
2. Break eggs one at a time into a saucer; when shortening begins to sputter slip eggs into pan.
3. Turn off heat; there is enough heat in pan to cook eggs until set. If you prefer to coat the eggs, cover pan with No. 843 cover.

VOGEL-HEU

    4 slices stale bread
    2 tablespoons butter
    4 eggs
    ½ cup milk
    ¼ teaspoon salt
    4 slices Swiss or yellow cream cheese, shredded

1. Toast bread; cut into bite-size squares.
2. Melt butter in No. 940 pan over low heat; place bread squares in pan; turn to coat evenly with butter.
3. Beat eggs; add milk, salt, cheese; stir.
4. Pour mixture over bread cubes; as eggs coagulate, stir, scrape from bottom of pan. Serve hot.
5. Two servings.

BACON CHEESE ROLLUPS

    4 slices bacon
    8 eggs
    4 tablespoons milk
    4 tablespoons shredded sharp cheese

1. Heat No. 918 pan over medium heat; broil bacon until crisp. Do not discard fat.
2. Beat eggs; add milk; pour into pan into a long strip about 2 inches wide. Cook until fairly firm. Sprinkle with grated cheese; place one bacon strip in center; roll up as for jelly roll. Move to one end of pan to keep hot while preparing remaining 3 rolls.
3. Four servings.

STUFFINGS

BREAD STUFFING

    6 tablespoons butter
    1/2 cup chopped celery
    2 tablespoons minced onion
    2 tablespoons chopped parsley
    4 cups cubed bread
      (approximately 12 slices)
    1/2 teaspoon sage or poultry seasoning
    1 teaspoon salt
    1/4 teaspoon pepper

1. Melt butter; add chopped celery, onion, parsley. Cook together three minutes; add bread, seasonings; toss.
2. Stuff chicken. The neck pocket will hold about 3/4 cup stuffing; the body the rest.
3. Yield: Stuffing for 4 pound chicken.

OYSTER STUFFING

    1 cup stewing oysters, chopped
    4 cups stale bread, cubed
    2 teaspoons salt
    1/8 teaspoon pepper
    1/8 teaspoon sage
    3 tablespoons butter
    1 onion, minced
    2 tablespoons finely chopped parsley
    3/4 cup finely chopped celery

1. Chop oysters coarsely; put into vegetable pan; cover; place over medium heat 5 minutes; reduce heat to low. Cook 4-5 minutes or until edges of oysters curl.
2. Drain well; save liquor if desired, for use in gravy.
3. Place bread cubes in bowl; add salt, pepper, sage; toss lightly to mix.
4. In No. 940 pan place butter, onion, parsley, celery. Cover; place over medium heat 5 minutes; reduce heat to low; cook 5-7 minutes or until onion is clear. Remove cover; brown lightly.
5. Pour over seasoned bread; toss together to mix well. Add oysters; mix.
6. Stuff chicken.
7. Yield: Stuffing for 4 pound chicken.

TURKEY STUFFING

    1/2 pound pork shoulder
    2 tablespoons butter
    1/2 cup chopped celery
    2 tablespoons onion, minced
    2 tablespoons parsley
    1 cup diced raw apples
    1/2 cup seedless raisins
    3 quarts cubed bread
    1/2 teaspoon poultry seasoning
    1 teaspoon salt
    1/4 teaspoon pepper

1. Stew pork until tender. Cut into cubes.
2. Melt butter in No. 940 pan; cook celery, onion, parsley in butter three minutes. Add apples, raisins, bread, seasonings; toss lightly.
3. Stuff turkey; skewer.
4. Yield: Stuffing for 12 pound turkey.

MUSHROOM STUFFING

    2 cups finely diced celery
    2 cups boiling water
    1/2 cup butter
    1/4 cup minced onion
    1/2 minced green pepper
    1/4 pound sliced mushrooms
    4 cups cubed bread
    4 teaspoons rubbed sage
    2 teaspoons salt
    1/2 teaspoon pepper

1. Simmer celery in boiling water 15-20 minutes; drain; reserve 1/2 cup liquor.
2. Melt butter in No. 940 pan; sauté onion, pepper, mushrooms until tender but not brown.
3. Mix bread, seasonings together; add celery, liquor, onion, green pepper, mushrooms; mix thoroughly.
4. Fill cavity of chicken lightly; secure opening; roast.
5. Yield: Stuffing for 4 pound chicken.

WILD RICE STUFFING

½ cup raw wild rice
1¼ cups boiling water
Giblets from fowl
1 tablespoon butter
1 small onion, chopped
¼ pound sausage meat
1 teaspoon salt
½ teaspoon dried sage

1. Put rice, water in No. 802 pan.

2. Place 2 quarts boiling water in bottom of No. 844 pan; place No. 807 ring in No. 844 pan; place No. 802 pan on ring; cover; steam 10 minutes; drain rice.

3. Clean; wash, chop giblets.

4. Melt butter in No. 940 pan; sauté giblets, onion, sausage 10 minutes; add cooked rice, salt, sage; cook 2 minutes longer.

5. Stuff cavity of pheasant.

SAUCES

GIBLET GRAVY

1. Simmer giblets; neck, tips of wings in 2½ cups salted water 30 minutes. Remove giblets; chop fine.

2. Brown 4 tablespoons fat in bottom of roaster; blend 4 tablespoons flour in fat; add 2 cups stock from giblets; simmer, stirring constantly until thick; add giblets; cook 5 minutes.

CHESTNUT STUFFING

½ pound chestnuts
1 tablespoon butter
½ pound sausage meat
¼ cup minced onion
½ cup hot water
1 teaspoon dried sage
1½ teaspoons salt
⅛ teaspoon pepper
4 cups cubed bread

1. Wash chestnuts; make a long slit through shell on both sides of chestnut; bake in very hot (500°F.) oven 15 minutes. Remove from oven; remove shells, skin. Boil chestnuts in salted water to cover 20 minutes; drain; chop fine.

2. Melt butter in No. 940 pan; sauté sausage, onion until sausage is thoroughly cooked.

3. Add water, sage, salt, pepper, bread crumbs, chestnuts; toss lightly.

4. Yield: Stuffing for 4 pound fowl.

SAVORY GRAVY WITH MUSHROOMS

Juice from roast
1½ cups finely chopped mushrooms
¼ cup flour
2½ cups cold water
1 teaspoon salt
⅛ teaspoon pepper
½ teaspoon Worcestershire sauce

1. Drain juice from roast; skim off 3 tablespoons fat; return to No. 844 pan; add mushrooms; brown lightly, about 8-9 minutes.

2. Dissolve flour in 1 cup cold water; stir until smooth or beat with rotary egg beater until smooth; add remainder of water.

3. When mushrooms are browned, add juice, flour-water mixture, stirring constantly until mixture is thickened.

4. Add salt, pepper, Worcestershire sauce; mix. Simmer slowly 5 minutes.

BROWN GRAVY

1. Remove meat from pan to warm platter. Skim off fat from juice remaining in pan. Return 3 tablespoons fat to juice.
2. Dissolve 3 tablespoons flour in 1/2 cup cold water; add to juice in roaster; stir well. Simmer until of desired thickness. Season to taste.

BARBECUE SAUCE

2 tablespoons butter
1 onion, chopped fine
1 clove garlic, minced
1/2 cup chopped celery
3/4 cup water
1 cup catsup
2 tablespoons vinegar
2 tablespoons lemon juice
2 tablespoons Worcestershire sauce
2 tablespoons brown sugar
1 teaspoon dry mustard
1 teaspoon salt
1/4 teaspoon pepper

1. Melt butter; add onion, garlic, celery; cook until tender.
2. Add remaining ingredients; simmer 20 minutes.

SHRIMP SAUCE

2 tablespoons butter
2 tablespoons flour
1/8 teaspoon black pepper
1/2 teaspoon salt
1 cup milk
1 teaspoon Worcestershire sauce
1/2 cup diced, cooked shrimp

1. Melt butter in vegetable pan.
2. Add flour, pepper, salt; blend until smooth.
3. Add milk gradually, stirring constantly.
4. Cook over low heat until smooth, thickened.
5. Add Worcestershire sauce, shrimp.
6. Serve over halibut steaks.

SPANISH SAUCE

2 tablespoons shortening
1 tablespoon minced lean raw ham
1 tablespoon chopped celery
1 tablespoon chopped carrot
1 tablespoon chopped onion
2 tablespoons flour
1/2 cup stock
1/2 cup tomato juice
1/2 teaspoon salt
1/8 teaspoon pepper

1. Melt shortening; add ham, vegetables; cook until browned.
2. Add flour, stock, tomato juice; cook until smooth.
3. Season with salt, pepper. Serve over smoked tongue.

SEA FOOD COCKTAIL SAUCE

1 tablespoon horseradish
1/2 cup chili sauce
2 tablespoons vinegar
1 teaspoon Worcestershire sauce
1/4 teaspoon celery salt

1. Mix in order given; chill; serve.
2. Allow approximately 2 tablespoons sauce per serving.
3. For variety, 1/2 cup finely diced celery may be used instead of celery salt or 2 tablespoons pickle relish may be added.

YUKON SAUCE

3 tablespoons butter
5 tablespoons flour
2 cups boiling water
1/4 cup butter (cut into small pieces)
1/2 teaspoon salt
1 tablespoon lemon juice
1 tablespoon finely chopped parsley

1. Melt butter in vegetable pan.
2. Add flour; blend well.
3. Add water gradually, stirring constantly; cook until smooth or of medium thickness.
4. Beat in butter.
5. Season with salt, lemon juice, parsley.

MEAT, POULTRY AND FISH BUYING GUIDE

Meat	Characteristics of Good Quality	Amount to Allow Per Serving	Amount to Buy	Pan to Use
Beef	Color purplish brown when first cut, changing rapidly to bright cherry red when exposed to air; lean, firm, fine grained, well marked with fat; bones red and porous; fat white, brittle, flaked.	Boned and rolled— ¼ pound Ground— ¼ pound With bone— ½ pound Canned, cooked, boneless meats—3 ounces Chipped dried beef— 1½ ounces For meat stock—Allow 3 pounds raw meat to 1 gallon stock	Multiply Amount to Allow per Serving by number to be served	Large roasts....844 Small roasts....940 Large steaks....918 Medium steaks..940 Small steaks....938
Veal	Color light greyish pink; lean, firm, fine grained, well marked with fat; fat white, firm, free from fiber; bones slightly pink.	Boned and rolled— ¼ pound Ground— ¼ pound With bone— ½ pound	Multiply Amount to Allow per Serving by number to be served	Large roasts....844 Small roasts....940 Large cutlets....918 4–8 chops or medium cutlets..940 1–3 chops......938
Pork (Fresh)	Color light greyish pink; lean, firm, fine grained, well marbled with fat; fat white, firm, free from fibers; bones slightly pink.	Boned and rolled— ¼ pound Ground— ¼ pound With bone— ½ pound	Multiply Amount to Allow per Serving by number to be served	Large roasts....844 Small roasts....940 Many chops....918 4–8 chops....940 1–3 chops......938
Pork (Smoked)	Color rich pink; lean, fine grained, well marbled with fat and a good layer of fat on outside; bone small.	Boned and rolled— ¼ pound Ground— ¼ pound With bone— ½ pound Boned and cooked— 2–3 ounces Bacon, sliced—2 ounces	Multiply Amount to Allow per Serving by number to be served	Large roasts....844 Small roasts....940 2 large steaks...918 Average steak...940
Lamb	Color dull pink; lean, firm, fine grained, tender, well marbled with fat; fat firm, white, thin and weblike; bones soft and red.	Boned and rolled— ¼ pound Ground— ¼ pound With bone— ½ pound Meat stock—allow 3 pounds raw meat to 1 gallon stock	Multiply Amount to Allow per Serving by number to be served	Large roasts....844 Small roasts....940 Many chops....918 4–10 chops.....940 1–3 chops......938
Chicken and Capon	Skin smooth, unbroken, moist; legs smooth and soft; fat distributed evenly; breast bone pliable.	Drawn weight— Broilers—1–2 pounds Fryers—1 pound Roasters or Stewers ½–¾ pound	Multiply Amount to Allow per Serving by number to be served	Roasting.......844 Frying...940 or 918
Duck	Breast firm, thick, tender; breastbone and bill pliable.	Drawn weight 1 pound	Multiply Amount to Allow per Serving by number to be served	Roasting.......844
Fish (Fresh)	Firm flesh; bright eyes; fresh odor.	Whole— ½ pound Fillets— ⅓ pound Steaks— ⅓ pound	Multiply Amount to Allow per Serving by number to be served	Baking.........844 Pan Broiling....940 or 938

top of range baking

845 Cover

837 Cake Tube

817 Steamer Plate

802 Inner Pan

843 Cover

807 Ring

844 Pan

940 Broiler Pan

818 Cover

918 Utility Pan

825 Combination Roaster

843
940

For direct heat top of range baking of loaf and upside down cake, biscuit, cinnamon roll, cornbread.

843

837

844

For angel, sponge, chiffon or butter cakes.

818
918

For direct heat top of range baking of large single layer cake, jelly roll, angel roll.

825

As an oven for baking pies, cakes, cookies, quickbreads, yeast breads.

845
802
817
844

For small loaf cake, fruit cake, nut bread.

WEAR-EVER NEW METHOD UTENSILS FOR...

top of range baking

79

top of range baking

No. 825 Large Rectangular Roaster as an Oven

1. Place No. 825 bottom pan inside middle section with control valve in rear.
2. Place lifting rack in bottom pan.
3. Adjust cover with heat control valve to front. It is necessary for the two heat control valves to be at opposite ends to permit proper circulation of heat.
4. The heat control valves in bottom pan and cover should remain open throughout entire baking period.
5. These directions apply only to the No. 825 roaster when used for baking.
6. Do not use on Controlled Heat unit.

To Create a "Slow" Oven (Approximately 275°F.-325°F.)
1. Arrange No. 825 roaster according to directions "1" through "4."
2. Place over medium heat; preheat 15 minutes.
3. Place food on rack.
4. Reduce heat to low at once.

To Create a "Moderate" Oven (Approximately 325°F.-375°F.)
1. Arrange No. 825 roaster according to directions "1" through "4."
2. Place over high heat; preheat 10 minutes.
3. Place food on rack.
4. Reduce heat to medium at once.

To Create a "Hot" Oven (Approximately 375°F.-450°F.)
1. Arrange No. 825 roaster according to directions "1" through "4."
2. Place over high heat; preheat 15 minutes.
3. Place food on rack.
4. Reduce heat to medium at once.

7. Times for preheating and heats used must be carefully controlled to prevent damage to the roaster. Dry metal subjected to high heat for a long period of time may be seriously damaged.

8. Two eight-inch layers of cake can be baked in the No. 825 roaster. Place one layer on lifting rack at one end. Place an aluminum measuring cup or similar support on lifting rack at other end and put second layer on this support. Be sure there is at least one inch of space around both pans. This permits free circulation of heat essential to even baking and browning.

Direct Heat Top of Range Baking

1. All types of cakes and quick breads are successfully done by Direct Heat Top of Range Baking. To bake on Controlled Heat unit see chart, page 13.
2. The regular New Method utensils No. 844, No. 845 and No. 940 can be used in combination or with No. 843 cover. The No. 918 utility pan and No. 818 cover may also be used depending on type of cake desired and amount of batter used.
3. Unless recipe states otherwise, grease pan; pour batter into pan; cover.
4. Place over <u>medium</u> heat 5 minutes.
5. Reduce heat to <u>low</u>; bake required time.

CAKES

MILK CHOCOLATE CAKE

½ cup shortening
1½ cups sugar
2 eggs
2 squares unsweetened chocolate, melted
2 cups sifted cake flour
½ teaspoon salt
1 teaspoon vanilla
1 cup sour milk or buttermilk
1 teaspoon soda
1 tablespoon vinegar

1. Cream shortening; add sugar; beat.
2. Add eggs, one at a time; beat well.
3. Add melted chocolate; blend.
4. Sift flour, salt together.
5. Add vanilla to sour milk.
6. Alternately add dry and liquid ingredients; blend until smooth.
7. Dissolve soda in vinegar; add last.
8. Put into greased No. 940 pan; cover with No. 843 cover; bake according to directions for Direct Heat Top of Range Baking.
9. Time: 60-65 minutes.

SOUR CREAM DEVIL'S FOOD CAKE

⅓ cup shortening
1¼ cups sugar
1 egg, unbeaten
1 teaspoon vanilla
3 squares unsweetened chocolate, melted
2 cups sifted cake flour
1 teaspoon soda
¾ teaspoon salt
½ cup thick sour cream
¾ cup sweet milk

1. Cream shortening; add sugar; beat until light, fluffy.
2. Add egg, vanilla; beat thoroughly.
3. Add melted chocolate; blend.
4. Sift dry ingredients together; add alternately dry and liquid ingredients; blend until smooth.
5. Put into greased No. 940 pan; cover with No. 843 cover; bake according to directions for Direct Heat Top of Range Baking.
6. Time: 45-50 minutes.

DARK DEVIL'S FOOD CAKE

- 1/2 cup shortening
- 1 1/4 cups brown sugar
- 3 eggs
- 6 squares unsweetened chocolate, melted
- 2 cups sifted cake flour
- 1 teaspoon soda
- 1 teaspoon salt
- 1 teaspoon baking powder
- 1 teaspoon vanilla
- 1 1/4 cups milk

1. Cream shortening; add sugar; beat.
2. Add eggs, one at a time; beat well.
3. Add melted chocolate; blend.
4. Sift dry ingredients together.
5. Add vanilla to milk.
6. Alternately add dry and liquid ingredients; blend until smooth.
7. Put into greased No. 940 pan; cover with No. 843 cover; bake according to directions for Direct Heat Top of Range Baking.
8. Time: 45-50 minutes.

COCONUT SILVER CAKE

- 1/2 cup butter
- 1 cup sugar
- 1 teaspoon vanilla
- 2 cups sifted cake flour
- 2 teaspoons baking powder
- 1/2 teaspoon salt
- 2/3 cup milk
- 3 stiffly beaten egg whites

1. Cream butter; add sugar, vanilla; cream until light, fluffy.
2. Sift together dry ingredients; add alternately with milk; mix well.
3. Fold in stiffly beaten egg whites.
4. Put into greased No. 940 pan; cover with No. 843 cover; bake according to directions for Direct Heat Top of Range Baking.
5. Spread with boiled frosting.
6. Sprinkle with coconut.
7. Time: 40-45 minutes.

BUTTER CREAM CAKE

- 1/3 cup butter
- 1 cup sugar
- 2 eggs
- 2 cups sifted cake flour
- 2 teaspoons baking powder
- 1/2 teaspoon salt
- 1 teaspoon vanilla
- 2/3 cup milk

1. Cream butter; add sugar; beat.
2. Add eggs, one at time; beat well.
3. Sift flour, baking powder, salt together.
4. Add vanilla to milk.
5. Alternately add dry and liquid ingredients; blend until smooth.
6. Put into greased No. 940 pan; cover with No. 843 cover; bake according to directions for Direct Heat Top of Range Baking.
7. Time: 40-45 minutes.

APPLESAUCE CAKE

- 2 eggs
- 1/2 cup shortening
- 1 cup sugar
- 3/4 cup thick unsweetened applesauce
- 1 1/2 cups sifted cake flour
- 1 teaspoon cinnamon
- 1/2 teaspoon nutmeg
- 1/4 teaspoon cloves
- 1/4 teaspoon allspice
- 1/2 teaspoon salt
- 2 teaspoons baking powder
- 1/2 cup chopped walnuts

1. Beat eggs until thick.
2. Cream shortening; add sugar; beat until light, fluffy.
3. Add beaten eggs, applesauce: mix.
4. Sift dry ingredients together; add; beat until smooth.
5. Fold in chopped walnuts.
6. Put into greased No. 940 pan; cover with No. 843 cover; bake according to directions for Direct Heat Top of Range Baking.
7. Time: 40-45 minutes.

PINEAPPLE UPSIDE DOWN CAKE

    ½ cup shortening
    1 cup sugar
    2 eggs
    2 cups sifted cake flour
    3 teaspoons baking powder
    ½ teaspoon salt
    1 teaspoon vanilla
    ¾ cup cold water
    1 cup brown sugar
    ¼ cup butter
    5 slices pineapple
    5 maraschino cherries

1. Cream shortening; add sugar; beat.
2. Add eggs, one at a time; beat well.
3. Sift flour, baking powder, salt together.
4. Add vanilla to water.
5. Alternately add dry and liquid ingredients; blend until smooth.
6. Grease No. 940 pan; sprinkle with brown sugar; dot with butter.
7. Arrange pineapple slices in pan; place cherry in center of each slice.
8. Spread cake batter evenly over pineapple; cover with No. 843 cover; bake according to directions for Direct Heat Top of Range Baking.
9. Time: 50-55 minutes.
10. Allow to stand covered 5 minutes before turning cake upside down on platter.
11. Serve with whipped cream.

CHOCOLATE BROWNIES

    1 cup and 2 tablespoons butter
    6 squares unsweetened chocolate
    2¼ cups sugar
    5 eggs, beaten
    2 teaspoons vanilla
    1¾ cups sifted cake flour
    1 teaspoon salt
    1 cup nuts, chopped coarsely

1. Melt shortening, chocolate together in No. 771 pan over low heat.
2. Add sugar, eggs, vanilla; beat until well blended.
3. Sift flour, salt together; mix with nuts; add last.
4. Put into greased No. 918 pan to ½ inch depth; cover with No. 818 cover.
5. Bake over <u>medium</u> heat 5 minutes; reduce heat to <u>low</u>; continue baking 20-25 minutes.
6. While still warm cut into 2 inch squares. These brownies should have a shiny top and a fudge-like center.
7. Yield: 5 dozen.

SOUR MILK GINGERBREAD

    ½ cup shortening
    ½ cup brown sugar
    2 eggs, beaten
    ½ cup molasses
    1½ cups sifted cake flour
    1 teaspoon baking powder
    1 teaspoon ginger
    1 teaspoon cinnamon
    ½ teaspoon nutmeg
    ½ teaspoon cloves
    1 teaspoon soda
    ¾ cup sour milk or buttermilk
    ½ cup sifted cake flour
    1 cup seedless raisins
    1 cup chopped nuts

1. Cream shortening; add sugar; beat.
2. Add eggs, molasses; mix.
3. Sift flour, baking powder, spices together.
4. Dissolve soda in milk.
5. Alternately add dry and liquid ingredients; blend until smooth.
6. Sift flour over raisins, nuts; add; mix thoroughly.
7. Put into greased No. 940 pan; cover with No. 843 cover; bake according to directions for Direct Heat Top of Range Baking.
8. Time: 45-55 minutes.

PRIZE SPICE CAKE

    6 tablespoons shortening
    1 cup brown sugar
    2 eggs
    1½ cups sifted cake flour
    ½ teaspoon baking powder
    ¼ teaspoon salt
    ¼ teaspoon cloves
    ½ teaspoon nutmeg
    1 teaspoon cinnamon
    ½ teaspoon vanilla
    ¾ teaspoon soda
    ½ cup sour milk or buttermilk

1. Cream shortening; add sugar; beat.
2. Add eggs, one at a time; beat well.
3. Sift dry ingredients together except soda.
4. Add vanilla, soda to sour milk.
5. Alternately add dry and liquid ingredients; blend until smooth.
6. Put into greased No. 940 pan; cover with No. 843 cover; bake according to directions for Direct Heat Top of Range Baking.
7. Time: 25-30 minutes.

MINCEMEAT FRUIT CAKE

    1 pound mincemeat
    1 cup seedless raisins
    1 cup chopped nuts
    1 cup sugar
    ½ cup shortening, melted
    1 teaspoon vanilla
    2 egg yolks
    2 cups sifted all purpose flour
    1½ teaspoons baking powder
    ½ teaspoon baking soda
    ½ teaspoon salt
    2 stiffly beaten egg whites

1. Mix mincemeat, raisins, nuts, sugar, shortening, vanilla, egg yolks; beat thoroughly.
2. Add sifted dry ingredients.
3. Fold in egg whites.
4. Put into greased No. 940 pan; cover with No. 843 cover.
5. Bake over <u>low</u> heat 2 hours.

BANANA NUT CAKE

    6 tablespoons butter
    ¾ cup sugar
    1 teaspoon vanilla
    2 egg yolks, well beaten
    ½ cup banana pulp
        (1-1½ bananas)
    ½ cup chopped walnuts
    1½ cups sifted cake flour
    1¼ teaspoons baking powder
    ¼ teaspoon baking soda
    ½ teaspoon salt
    ½ cup buttermilk
    1 stiffly beaten egg white

1. Cream butter; add sugar, vanilla; cream until light, fluffy.
2. Add egg yolks.
3. Make banana pulp by putting through food press.
4. Add banana pulp, walnuts; mix.
5. Sift together dry ingredients; add alternately with milk; mix well.
6. Fold in stiffly beaten egg white.
7. Put into greased No. 940 pan; cover with No. 843 cover; bake according to directions for Direct Heat Top of Range Baking.
8. Time: 40-45 minutes.

CREAM SPONGE CAKE

    4 egg whites
    ½ cup sugar
    4 egg yolks
    2 tablespoons cold water
    1 teaspoon vanilla
    ½ cup sugar
    1 cup sifted cake flour
    1½ tablespoons cornstarch
    1¼ teaspoons baking powder
    ¼ teaspoon salt

1. Beat egg whites until stiff, but not dry; add sugar; beat thoroughly.
2. Beat egg yolks, water, vanilla until lemon colored; add sugar; beat until well blended.
3. Fold two mixtures together.
4. Sift dry ingredients together; fold into mixture with wooden spoon.

5. Put into No. 940 pan; cover with No. 843 cover; bake according to directions for Direct Heat Top of Range Baking.
6. Time: 45-50 minutes.

ORANGE CHIFFON CAKE

    2¼ cups sifted cake flour
    1½ cups sugar
       3 teaspoons baking powder
       1 teaspoon salt
    ½ cup salad oil
       5 unbeaten egg yolks
       2 tablespoons grated orange rind
       Juice of 2 oranges + juice of 1 lemon + water to make ¾ cup
       1 cup egg whites
    ½ teaspoon cream of tartar

1. Sift dry ingredients into bowl. Make a well; add in order oil, egg yolks, rind, liquid; beat until smooth.
2. Beat egg whites, cream of tartar until very stiff.
3. Pour egg yolk mixture over egg whites; fold gently just until blended. Do not stir.
4. Put No. 837 cake tube into center of No. 844 pan.
5. Pour batter around cake tube; cover; bake over a very low heat 65-70 minutes or until done.
6. Invert pan; allow cake to cool.
7. Loosen with spatula; turn onto rack.

SMALL ORANGE CHIFFON CAKE

1. Use one-half recipe given above.
2. Mix according to above directions.
3. Put into No. 940 pan; cover.
4. Bake over medium-low heat 5 minutes; reduce heat to low; continue baking 20-25 minutes or until done.
5. Invert pan; allow cake to cool.
6. Loosen with spatula; turn onto rack.

CHOCOLATE SPONGE ROLL

    6 tablespoons sifted cake flour
    ½ teaspoon baking powder
    ¼ teaspoon salt
    4 eggs, separated
    ¾ cup sugar
    1 teaspoon vanilla
    2 squares unsweetened chocolate, melted

1. Sift flour, baking powder, salt together.
2. Beat egg whites, sugar until stiff.
3. Beat egg yolks, vanilla until thick.
4. Fold egg yolks into egg whites.
5. Fold dry ingredients into mixture; add melted chocolate; blend.
6. Grease No. 918 pan; line bottom with brown paper. Pour in mixture.
7. Cover with No. 818 cover.
8. Bake over low heat 15-20 minutes.
9. Cut off crisp edges; turn onto cloth; remove paper; quickly roll; cool.
10. Unroll; spread with Boiled Icing, ice cream or fruit filling; reroll.

ANGEL FOOD CAKE

    1 cup sifted cake flour
    1¼ cups sugar
    ¼ teaspoon salt
    1 cup egg whites
    ¾ teaspoon cream of tartar
    1 teaspoon vanilla
    ¼ teaspoon almond extract

1. Sift flour, sugar and salt together nine times.
2. Beat egg whites with wire whip until frothy.
3. Add cream of tartar, continue beating until eggs are stiff but not dry. Add extract and beat one minute longer.
4. Fold in dry ingredients, about 4 tablespoons at a time, using a wooden spoon. Fold only until dry ingredients disappear in mixture. Do not handle batter any more than necessary.
5. Pour into ungreased No. 844 pan fitted with No. 837 cake tube; cover with No. 843 cover.
6. Bake over very low heat one hour or until done.

WHITE FRUIT CAKE

2½ cups sifted all purpose flour
1½ teaspoons baking powder
¾ teaspoon salt
1 cup shortening
1 cup sugar
5 eggs
¾ cup pineapple or orange juice
1 cup diced apricots
1 cup seedless raisins
⅓ cup chopped candied orange peel
⅓ cup chopped citron
¾ cup sliced figs
¾ cup chopped dates
1 cup chopped candied pineapple
1 cup chopped blanched almonds
1 teaspoon grated lemon rind
¾ cup candied cherries, cut into halves

1. Sift flour, measure. Measure ½ cup flour, set aside for coating fruit.
2. Sift together remaining flour, baking powder, salt.
3. Cream shortening, add sugar gradually; beat until light, fluffy. Add eggs one at a time; beat after each addition.
4. Add dry ingredients alternately with juice; beat until smooth.
5. Coat fruits, nuts with the ½ cup flour; fold in thoroughly.
6. Pour into well greased loaf pans. If desired, the No. 802 pan can be used. Pans should be three-fourths full.
7. Steam bake in No. 825 roaster according to directions.
8. Yield: 5½-6 pounds.

TO STEAM BAKE FRUIT CAKE

1. Adjust lifting rack in No. 825 roaster. Pour water into bottom of roaster until it comes up to bottom of lifting rack. Top of rack should remain dry. Place slice of lemon in water. This prevents discoloration.
2. Place pans of fruit cake on lifting rack. Be sure there is at least one inch free space around each pan so heat will circulate freely.
3. Adjust roaster cover; close vents.
4. Place over medium heat until water comes to a boil and roaster is filled with steam. Reduce heat to low. Steam bake:
   1—2 pound cakes—2½ hours
   3—5 pound cakes—3½-4 hours
5. Check every hour to make sure water in bottom pan has not all evaporated. Add more water if necessary, but be sure it does not come up to top of lifting rack.
6. When steam baking time is up, remove lifting rack with cakes. Dry bottom pan.
7. Assemble No. 825 roaster as oven. Open vent in bottom pan.
8. Heat No. 825 roaster according to directions for very "Slow" (275°F.) oven.
9. When oven has reached temperature place cakes on lifting rack.
10. Adjust cover; open vent in cover one-half way; bake 1½ hours.
11. Test for doneness by inserting toothpick or cake tester into cake. If done, tester will come out clean.
12. Cool cake on rack; wrap closely; store.

ICINGS
BOILED ICING

1 cup sugar
2 egg whites (unbeaten)
4 tablespoons cold water
¼ teaspoon cream of tartar
½ teaspoon vanilla

1. Fit No. 807 ring into No. 844 pan; put 5 cups water into pan; bring to boil.
2. Place sugar, egg whites, water, cream of tartar in No. 802 pan.
3. Set over boiling water; with rotary egg beater, beat until icing will hang in a point when lifted above pan (12 minutes.)
4. Add vanilla; blend; spread on cake.
5. If desired, three squares melted unsweetened chocolate may be added to ingredients.

BUTTER CREAM ICING

    1 tablespoon butter
    1 cup confectioner's sugar
    1 tablespoon milk
    1 teaspoon vanilla

1. Melt butter; add sugar, milk, vanilla.
2. Beat well; spread on cake.

Variations: One square melted unsweetened chocolate may be added. Or, substitute orange juice for one-half milk and add ½ teaspoon grated orange rind.

SEA FOAM TOPPING

    2 egg whites
    1½ cups brown sugar, firmly packed
    5 tablespoons cold water
    Dash of salt
    1 teaspoon vanilla

1. Combine egg whites, sugar, cold water, salt; beat until thoroughly mixed.
2. Place over rapidly boiling water, continuing to beat until mixture peaks on beater.
3. Remove from boiling water; add vanilla; mix.
4. Spread on cake.

FUDGE ICING

    3 cups sugar
    3 squares unsweetened chocolate
    ¼ teaspoon cream of tartar
    1 cup milk
    2 tablespoons butter
    2 egg yolks
    1 teaspoon vanilla

1. Mix all except egg yolks and vanilla together.
2. Bring to boil; cook to soft ball stage.
3. Pour slowly over egg yolks; beat until creamy; add vanilla; spread on cake.

MIRACLE ICING

    1 cup sugar
    1 egg white, unbeaten
    ¼ teaspoon cream of tartar
    ½ cup boiling water
    1 teaspoon vanilla

1. Mix sugar, egg white, cream of tartar together.
2. Add boiling water; beat on high speed of electric mixer until stiff.
3. Add vanilla; spread on cake.

MINT BUTTER CREAM ICING

    2 tablespoons butter
    2 cups confectioner's sugar
    1 teaspoon vanilla
    1 tablespoon milk
    6 tablespoons mint jelly

1. Cream butter; add sugar, vanilla, milk, mint jelly. Beat until smooth.
2. Spread on cake. If desired, sprinkle with chocolate sprinkles.

CHOCOLATE CONFECTIONERS' FROSTING

1. Melt ¼ cup butter or margarine, 1½ ounces unsweetened chocolate over <u>low</u> heat.
2. Remove from heat; add 2 tablespoons hot water, ½ teaspoon vanilla, a few grains salt, 2 cups sifted confectioners' sugar.
3. Stir until smooth, glossy, adding a few drops of water, if necessary, to keep soft.

PIES

FLAKY PIE CRUST

    2¼ cups sifted all purpose flour
    ¾ teaspoon salt
    ¾ cup shortening
    5 tablespoons ice water

1. Sift flour, salt together.
2. Blend shortening with dry ingredients with pastry blender. (Mixture will become fine but will lump upon further blending.) Blend until all particles are the size of peas; chill in refrigerator 15 minutes or overnight.
3. Sprinkle water, a few drops at a time, over mixture; work it in lightly with a fork until all particles are moistened and in small lumps.
4. Empty contents of bowl onto waxed paper; press into a ball; chill about ½ hour.
5. Roll crust on floured board with quick light strokes.
6. Fit gently into pan; removing all air bubbles; trim overhang to 1½ inches; fold edge underneath between pastry and rim of pan.
7. Flute edges with fingers.
8. Brush shell with unbeaten egg white.
9. Makes 1 nine-inch double crust pie or 2 single crust pies.

PUMPKIN PIE FILLING

    1½ cups milk
    1½ cups cooked pumpkin
    1¼ cups sugar
    1 teaspoon cinnamon
    ½ teaspoon nutmeg
    ½ teaspoon ginger
    ½ teaspoon salt
    2 eggs, well beaten

1. Mix ingredients in order listed.
2. Pour into 9 inch unbaked shell.
3. Assemble No. 825 roaster according to directions for "Hot" (425°F.) oven; place pie on lifting rack; cover; bake 40 minutes.
4. Six servings.

NEW METHOD CHERRY PIE

    1 cup sugar
    ¼ cup sifted pastry flour
    ¼ teaspoon nutmeg
    ⅛ teaspoon salt
    ¼ teaspoon cinnamon
    4 cups fresh pitted cherries
    1 teaspoon lemon juice
    1 tablespoon liquid red coloring
    1 tablespoon butter

1. Sift dry ingredients together; mix with cherries; add lemon juice, coloring.
2. Line 9 inch pie pan with pastry; brush bottom of pie crust with egg white; pour cherries into pie.
3. Dot with butter; cover with top crust.
4. Assemble No. 825 roaster according to directions for "Hot" (425°F.) oven; place pie on lifting rack; cover; bake 45 minutes.
5. Six servings.

DUTCH APPLE PIE

    Unbaked 9 inch pastry shell
    1 cup sugar
    ⅓ cup water
    ⅓ cup cream
    1 tablespoon butter
    ½ teaspoon cinnamon
    1 tablespoon flour
    1 tablespoon sugar
    1 egg white, slightly beaten
    4 cups tart apples, pared, cored, sliced ¼ inch thick

1. Boil sugar, water together 4-5 minutes to make heavy syrup. Add cream, butter, cinnamon. Allow to cool five minutes.
2. Blend flour, sugar together. Brush bottom of crust with egg white; sprinkle with flour, sugar. Place apples on top, cut side flat. Pour syrup mixture over apples being careful to coat all exposed pieces.
3. Assemble No. 825 roaster to create "Hot" (400°F.) oven; place pie on lifting rack; cover; bake 1 hour.
4. Six servings.

LEMON CHIFFON PIE

    1 envelope plain, unflavored gelatin
    1/4 cup cold water
    4 eggs, separated
    1 cup sugar
    1/2 cup lemon juice
    1/2 teaspoon salt
    1 teaspoon grated lemon rind
    1 baked 9 inch pie shell
    1/2 cup heavy cream, whipped

1. Soak gelatin in cold water 5 minutes.
2. Place 1 quart water in No. 844 pan; bring to boil.
3. Fit No. 807 ring on No. 844 pan.
4. Combine in No. 802 pan beaten egg yolks, 1/2 cup sugar, lemon juice, salt.
5. Cook over boiling water until smooth, thickened, stirring constantly.
6. Add gelatin; stir until dissolved; add lemon rind; chill until it begins to set.
7. Beat egg whites until stiff; gradually add remaining 1/2 cup sugar.
8. Fold into cooled custard mixture.
9. Pour into baked pie shell; chill until set.
10. Garnish with whipped cream just before serving.
11. Six servings.

COOKIES

PEANUT CRINKLES

    1/2 cup peanut butter
    1/4 cup butter
    1/2 cup brown sugar
    1/2 cup sugar
    1 egg, well beaten
    1 cup sifted cake flour
    1 teaspoon soda

1. Cream peanut butter, butter together; add sugars gradually; beat until light, fluffy.
2. Add egg; beat well.
3. Sift dry ingredients together; add to creamed mixture; beat thoroughly.
4. Drop by teaspoonfuls on sheet of Alcoa Wrap aluminum foil.
5. Press down each cookie with a four-tined fork. Press a second time so that creases are at right angles to those first made.
6. Assemble No. 825 roaster to create "Moderate" (350°F.) oven; place cookies on rack; cover; bake 12 minutes.
7. Yield: 4 1/2 dozen cookies.

FROSTED JUMBOS

    1 3/4 cups sifted all purpose flour
    2 teaspoons baking powder
    1/2 teaspoon salt
    1 egg
    1 cup light brown sugar
    1 teaspoon vanilla
    2 ounces melted, unsweetened chocolate
    1/2 cup salad oil or melted shortening
    1/2 cup milk
    1/2 cup shredded coconut
    Walnut or pecan halves

1. Sift dry ingredients together.
2. Beat egg until light; gradually add sugar; beat until fluffy.
3. Add vanilla, chocolate, shortening; mix well.
4. Add sifted dry ingredients alternately with milk, beating after each addition.
5. Stir in coconut.
6. Drop by teaspoonfuls on sheet of Alcoa Wrap aluminum foil.
7. Assemble No. 825 roaster to create a "Moderate" (350°F.) oven; place cookies on rack; cover; bake 12-15 minutes.
8. Cool. Swirl chocolate confectioners' frosting in center; top with half a walnut or pecan.
9. Yield: 1 1/2 dozen Jumbos.

BLACK WALNUT COOKIES

    1¾ cups butter
    1 pound brown sugar
    ½ cup sugar
    2 eggs, beaten
    1 teaspoon vanilla
    1 teaspoon black walnut extract
    1½ cups black walnuts
    1½ cups shredded coconut
    6 cups sifted cake flour
    1 teaspoon cream of tartar
    1 teaspoon salt
    ½ teaspoon soda

1. Cream butter; add sugars gradually; beat until light, fluffy.
2. Add eggs one at a time; beat after each addition. Add extracts; mix well.
3. Grind nuts, coconut together; combine with butter-sugar mixture; add sifted dry ingredients.
4. Shape into rolls; wrap in Alcoa Wrap aluminum foil; place in refrigerator to chill.
5. Slice thin; place on sheet of Alcoa Wrap aluminum foil.
6. Assemble No. 825 roaster to create "Moderate" (375°F.) oven; place cookies on rack; cover; bake 10-12 minutes.
7. This dough will keep several weeks if stored in refrigerator.

APRICOT COCONUT COOKIES

    ½ cup butter
    ¾ cup sugar
    1 egg, well beaten
    1 tablespoon grated orange rind
    2¼ cups sifted cake flour
    ½ teaspoon salt
    2½ teaspoons baking powder
    Juice of 1 medium orange
    Juice of 1 small lemon
    ½ cup dried apricots, chopped
    ½ cup shredded coconut
    ¼ cup chopped nuts

1. Cream butter; add sugar gradually; beat until light, fluffy. Add egg, grated orange rind; beat well.
2. Sift dry ingredients together.
3. Pour orange, lemon juice over apricots, coconut.
4. Alternately add dry, liquid ingredients to creamed mixture; blend.
5. Add chopped nuts; beat 30 seconds.
6. Drop by tablespoonfuls onto sheet of Alcoa Wrap aluminum foil about 2 inches apart.
7. Assemble No. 825 roaster to create a "Moderate" (375°F.) oven.
8. Place cookies on rack; cover; bake 10 minutes.
9. Yield: 4 dozen cookies.

CHRISTMAS CHERRIES

    ½ cup shortening
    ¼ cup sugar
    1 egg, separated
    1 tablespoon grated orange rind
    1½ teaspoons grated lemon rind
    ½ teaspoon vanilla
    1 tablespoon lemon juice
    1 cup sifted cake flour
    ¾ cup chopped walnuts
    6 candied cherries

1. Cream shortening; add sugar gradually; beat until light, fluffy.
2. Add egg yolk; beat thoroughly.
3. Add orange, lemon rind, vanilla, lemon juice; blend thoroughly.
4. Add flour; mix well; wrap in Alcoa Wrap aluminum foil; chill several hours.
5. Roll into small balls ½ inch in diameter; roll in slightly beaten egg white; then in chopped walnuts.
6. Place on sheet of Alcoa Wrap aluminum foil; press piece of cherry into each.
7. Assemble No. 825 roaster to create "Moderate" (350°F.) oven; place cookies on rack; cover; bake 20 minutes.
8. Yield: 33 cookies 1½ inches in diameter.

LEMON DROPS

    2 cups sifted all purpose flour
    ½ teaspoon baking soda
    ½ teaspoon salt
    ½ cup shortening
    1 cup sugar
    1 teaspoon vanilla
    2 eggs
    1 tablespoon grated lemon rind
    ¼ cup lemon juice
    ¼ cup sugar
    1½ teaspoons grated lemon rind

1. Sift dry ingredients together.
2. Cream shortening; add sugar; beat until light, fluffy.
3. Add vanilla, eggs; beat well.
4. Add sifted dry ingredients alternately with 1 tablespoon grated lemon rind, juice; beat well after each addition.
5. Drop by teaspoonfuls on sheet Alcoa Wrap aluminum foil.
6. Combine remaining sugar, lemon rind; sprinkle on center of each cookie.
7. Assemble No. 825 roaster to create "Moderate" (375°F.) oven; place cookies on rack; cover; bake 12-15 minutes.
8. Yield: 4½ dozen cookies.

SAND TARTS

    ½ cup shortening
    1 cup sugar
    1 egg, well beaten
    1 teaspoon grated orange rind
    1¾ cups sifted all purpose flour
    1 teaspoon baking powder
    ½ teaspoon salt

1. Cream shortening; add sugar gradually; beat until light, fluffy.
2. Add egg, orange rind.
3. Add sifted dry ingredients.
4. Chill dough; roll to ⅛ inch thickness; cut into fancy shapes.
5. Place on sheet of Alcoa Wrap aluminum foil; brush with unbeaten egg white diluted with water; sprinkle with cinnamon; decorate with almonds.
6. Assemble No. 825 roaster to create "Moderate" (350°F.) oven; place cookies on rack; cover; bake 10 minutes.
7. Yield: 3 dozen cookies.

QUICK BREADS
BAKING POWDER BISCUITS

    4 cups sifted all purpose flour
    6 teaspoons baking powder
    1 teaspoon salt
    1 tablespoon sugar
    6 tablespoons shortening
    1¼ cups milk (approximately)

1. Sift dry ingredients together.
2. Cut shortening into dry ingredients using a pastry blender or two silver knives.
3. Add milk slowly to make a soft sticky dough.
4. Turn dough on lightly floured board.
5. Flour hands, pat dough (do not use rolling pin) to ½ inch thickness.
6. Cut with biscuit cutter which has been dipped into flour.
7. Put into ungreased No. 940 pan; cover.
8. Place over low heat; bake 10 minutes.
9. Turn over biscuits; cover; bake 10 minutes longer.
10. Yield: 24 biscuits.

SAVORY BISCUITS

    1 cup sifted all purpose flour
    2 teaspoons baking powder
    ½ teaspoon salt
    1 tablespoon minced onion
    1 tablespoon minced parsley
    2 tablespoons shortening
    6 tablespoons milk

1. Sift dry ingredients together. Add onion, parsley, shortening. Blend with pastry blender or two knives.
2. Add liquid—enough to make a soft dough; mix with fork.
3. Pat out on floured board to ⅜ inch thickness. Cut with 1 inch biscuit cutter.
4. Bake on top of Oyster Pot Pie.

SCOTCH SCONES

    2 cups sifted all purpose flour
    4 teaspoons baking powder
    1 teaspoon salt
    4 tablespoons shortening
    ⅔ cup milk

1. Sift dry ingredients together.
2. Cut in shortening with pastry blender or two knives; add milk to make soft dough.
3. Toss on floured board. Pat into two round patties; roll ½ inch thick.
4. Cut each patty into six triangular sections.
5. Heat No. 918 pan over <u>high</u> heat until a small piece of white paper placed in the bottom turns brown; reduce heat to <u>medium</u>-<u>low</u>.
6. Bake scones on hot griddle until delicately browned on both sides. Allow 7-9 minutes per side.
7. Yield: 12 scones.

PLAIN MUFFINS

    2 cups sifted all purpose flour
    2 tablespoons sugar
    3 teaspoons baking powder
    1 teaspoon salt
    1 cup milk
    1 egg, beaten
    3 tablespoons melted shortening

1. Sift dry ingredients together.
2. Combine milk, egg.
3. Pour liquid ingredients into dry ingredients.
4. Stir <u>only</u> until flour is moistened.
5. Stir in melted shortening.
6. Fill greased muffin pans ⅔ full.
7. Assemble No. 825 roaster to create "Hot" (425°F.) oven; place on rack; cover; bake 20 minutes.
8. Yield: 12 muffins.

BACON, CHEESE AND TOMATO JUICE MUFFINS

    6 strips lean bacon
    2 cups sifted all purpose flour
    2 teaspoons baking powder
    1½ teaspoons salt
    2 tablespoons sugar
    ½ cup milk
    ½ cup tomato juice
    ¼ cup melted bacon fat
    1 egg, well beaten
    ¼ pound sharp yellow cheese, grated

1. Place bacon strips in cold No. 940 pan. Place over <u>medium</u> heat 5 minutes; reduce heat to <u>low</u>. Cook until done, turning frequently.
2. Drain bacon on paper toweling or piece of heavy brown paper. When well drained, break into bits.
3. Sift dry ingredients together.
4. Combine milk, tomato juice, melted bacon fat, egg.
5. Add to dry ingredients with chopped cooked bacon, grated yellow cheese. Beat just enough to blend.
6. Fill well greased muffin pans ⅔ full.
7. Assemble No. 825 roaster to create "Hot" (400°F.) oven; place on rack; cover; bake 15 minutes.
8. Yield: 12 muffins.

FLUFFY DUMPLINGS

    1 egg
    ¾ cup milk
    2 cups sifted all purpose flour
    3 teaspoons baking powder
    ½ teaspoon salt
    1 tablespoon butter, melted

1. Break egg into bowl; beat well; add milk, sifted dry ingredients; beat thoroughly.
2. Add melted butter. Drop by tablespoonfuls on top of stew.
3. Cover; cook 10 minutes over <u>low</u> heat.

FRENCH COFFEE CAKE

½ cup vegetable shortening
1 cup sugar
1 teaspoon vanilla
3 eggs, beaten
2 cups sifted all purpose flour
1 teaspoon baking powder
1 teaspoon baking soda
½ teaspoon salt
½ pint thick sour cream

Topping
2 tablespoons butter
3 tablespoons flour
¾ cup brown sugar
½ cup nuts, chopped fine

1. Cream shortening; add sugar gradually; beat until light, fluffy.
2. Add vanilla, eggs; beat well.
3. Sift dry ingredients together; alternately add dry and liquid ingredients; blend until smooth.
4. Cream butter, flour together for topping; add sugar; mix until crumbly; add nuts.
5. Put half of batter into No. 940 pan; cover with half the nut mixture; cover with other half of batter; sprinkle remaining nut mixture on top; sprinkle with cinnamon.
6. Cover; bake over very low heat 55-65 minutes or until done.

CINNAMON PECAN ROLLS

1 box hot roll mix
2 tablespoons soft butter
¾ cup light brown sugar
1½ teaspoons cinnamon
½ cup pecan nuts, chopped

1. Prepare dough according to directions on package.
2. Roll dough on lightly floured board to ¼ inch thickness. Spread with soft butter.
3. Mix together brown sugar, cinnamon, pecans. Sprinkle over surface of dough; roll up like jelly roll. Cut into 1 inch slices.
4. Butter No. 940 pan; pat ⅔ cup brown sugar into bottom of pan, sprinkle with ½ teaspoon cinnamon; dot with 2 tablespoons butter; add ¼ cup pecans. Place rolls on paste.
5. Allow to rise in warm place until double in bulk; cover.
6. Bake over medium heat 5 minutes; reduce heat to low; bake 17 minutes or until done.
7. Allow to stand 5 minutes before turning out upside down on cake rack.
8. Makes approximately 12-16 rolls.
9. Walnuts, raisins, almonds or a mixture of fruits and nuts may be substituted for the pecans in this recipe.

COFFEE CAKE

2 cups sifted all purpose flour
4 teaspoons baking powder
½ teaspoon salt
½ cup sugar
¼ cup shortening
1 egg, beaten
¾ cup milk
½ teaspoon vanilla

Topping
½ cup light brown sugar
2 teaspoons cinnamon
2 tablespoons flour
1 cup coarsely chopped walnuts
2 tablespoons melted shortening

1. Sift flour, baking powder, salt, sugar together three times.
2. Cut in shortening with pastry blender or two knives. Add egg, milk, vanilla.
3. Alternately add dry and liquid ingredients; mix well.
4. Put into greased No. 940 pan; cover with No. 843 cover; bake over medium heat 5 minutes; reduce heat to low; bake 10 minutes.
5. Combine ingredients for topping; mix well; sprinkle over cake; replace cover; continue baking 10 minutes.

CORN BREAD

    1¼ cups sifted all purpose flour
    3 teaspoons baking powder
    1 teaspoon salt
    1 tablespoon sugar
    1 cup corn meal (yellow or white)
    1 egg, beaten
    1 cup milk
    2 tablespoons melted shortening

1. Sift flour, baking powder, salt, sugar together; add corn meal; mix well.
2. Combine egg, milk, shortening; add to dry ingredients; mix.
3. Put into greased No. 940 or No. 918 pan; cover; bake over low heat 25-30 minutes.
4. Cut into squares; serve hot.

OLD-FASHIONED RICH DOUGHNUTS

    4 cups sifted all purpose flour
    4 teaspoons baking powder
    ½ teaspoon cinnamon
    ½ teaspoon salt
    ⅓ cup shortening
    4 egg yolks
    1 cup sugar
    1 cup milk
    Confectioner's or granulated sugar

1. Sift dry ingredients together.
2. Melt shortening. Beat egg yolks until very light, thick. Gradually beat in sugar.
3. Stir in milk, melted shortening.
4. Add flour mixture to egg mixture; mix thoroughly.
5. Roll out dough about ⅓ inch thick on lightly floured board; cut with doughnut cutter.
6. Melt about 1¾ pounds shortening in No. 940 pan. When thermometer reaches 365°F. or a cube of bread browns in one minute, fat is ready for frying. Drop doughnuts into hot fat; fry until light brown on one side; turn; fry other side. Drain on paper toweling, or brown paper. While still warm, "sugar" with either granulated or confectioners' sugar.
7. Yield: 24 doughnuts.

YEAST BREADS

BASIC REFRIGERATOR ROLLS

    1 cup hot water
    1 teaspoon salt
    6 tablespoons shortening
    ¼ cup sugar
    1 cake yeast
    2 tablespoons lukewarm water
    1 egg, well beaten
    3½-4 cups sifted all purpose flour

1. Combine hot water, salt, shortening, sugar in large bowl.
2. Cool to lukewarm; soften yeast in lukewarm water.
3. Add yeast, beaten egg, half the flour; beat well.
4. Stir in enough flour to make dough easy to handle.
5. Grease top of dough; cover; store in refrigerator.
6. Cut off dough as needed; shape into small balls; dip in melted butter; place three rolls in each section of greased muffin pan.
7. Cover; let rise in warm place until double in bulk.
8. Assemble No. 825 roaster to create "Hot" (425°F.) oven; place rolls on rack; cover; bake 12-15 minutes.
9. Yield: 18 rolls.

BUTTERSCOTCH ROLLS

    2¼ cups milk
    ½ cup shortening
    2 cakes yeast
    ¼ cup sugar
    2 eggs, well beaten
    7 cups sifted all purpose flour
    2½ teaspoons salt

1. Scald milk; melt shortening in hot milk; add sugar.
2. Cool milk to lukewarm; add yeast.
3. Add beaten eggs; beat in flour, salt to form soft dough.

4. Sprinkle dough with flour; pat into ball; wrap in Alcoa Wrap aluminum foil; set in refrigerator until 3 hours before baking.
5. Grease muffin pans heavily with vegetable shortening. For every dozen rolls mix 1 cup light brown sugar, ¼ cup butter. Put one tablespoon of mixture into bottom of each cup.
6. Roll dough into oblong shape about ¼ inch thick. Spread with melted butter, sprinkle with cinnamon. Roll into long roll; cut into 1 inch pieces. Place in muffin pans.
7. Put in warm place to rise 2-3 hours.
8. Assemble No. 825 roaster to create "Hot" (425°F.) oven; place rolls on rack; cover; bake 20 minutes.
9. Have large sheet of Alcoa Wrap aluminum foil ready to turn out rolls. Let rolls cool with "sticky" side up.
10. Yield: 3-4 dozen rolls.

ENGLISH MUFFINS

    3 tablespoons butter
    1¼ teaspoons salt
    2 tablespoons sugar
    1 cup milk, scalded
    1 cake yeast
    ¼ cup lukewarm water
    1 egg, beaten
    4 cups sifted all purpose flour

1. Add butter, salt, sugar to milk; cool.
2. Soften yeast in water; add yeast, egg, 2 cups flour to cooled milk; stir to blend well.
3. Knead in remaining flour until firm and elastic.
4. Let rise to double bulk; roll to ¼ inch thickness on floured board.
5. Cut into 4 inch circles; leave on board.
6. Cover; let rise until double in bulk.
7. Bake slowly on No. 918 utility pan over <u>low</u> heat 7 minutes to a side.
8. Yield: 12 muffins.

SOUR CREAM TWISTS

    4 cups sifted all purpose flour
    1 teaspoon salt
    1 cup shortening
    1 cake compressed yeast or
        1 envelope dry yeast
    ¼ cup lukewarm water
    1 egg, well beaten
    1 cup thick sour cream
    1 teaspoon vanilla
    ¾ cup sugar

1. Sift flour, salt together.
2. Cut shortening into flour until fat-flour particles are size of peas as for pie crust.
3. Dissolve yeast in lukewarm water; soak 5-10 minutes.
4. Mix yeast, egg, sour cream, vanilla together.
5. Combine dry, liquid ingredients; mix.
6. Put into greased bowl; cover; place in refrigerator to rise 2 hours.
7. Turn onto board sprinkled with sugar; roll into a large thin square; sprinkle with sugar again. Fold dough to center from each side; sprinkle with sugar; roll again; repeat folding operation, using more sugar. Do this four times, sprinkling sugar on board and dough to prevent sticking.
8. Cut into strips ¾ inch x 4 inches.
9. Sprinkle with sugar; shape into twists; place on a sheet of Alcoa Wrap aluminum foil.
10. Assemble No. 825 roaster to create "Moderate" (375°F.) oven; place twists on rack; cover; bake 20 minutes or until light brown.
11. Makes 3 dozen twists.
12. If you prefer, sprinkle dough with a mixture of
    1 cup finely chopped nuts
        (use food chopper)
    ½ cup brown sugar
    1 teaspoon cinnamon

before folding dough; roll again and sprinkle again with mixture as in direction No. 7. Bake according to directions for plain twists.

Directions for Use of No. 918 Utility Pan as Griddle

1. Heat over medium-high heat until a piece of white paper placed on griddle turns brown. Do not use on Controlled Heat unit.
2. Reduce heat to medium; pour cakes.
3. It is not necessary to use grease on the griddle if the heat is properly applied and the following recipes are used.

GRIDDLE CAKES

    1¼ cups sifted all purpose flour
    2½ teaspoons baking powder
    3 tablespoons sugar
    ¾ teaspoon salt
    1 egg
    1 cup sweet milk
    3 tablespoons butter, melted

1. Sift dry ingredients together.
2. Beat egg; add milk.
3. Stir into dry ingredients; mix.
4. Add melted butter.
5. Heat No. 918 pan over high heat until a piece of white paper placed in bottom turns brown.
6. Remove paper; reduce heat to medium; pour cakes.
7. Yield: 11 medium size cakes.

SOUR CREAM PANCAKES

    2 cups sifted all purpose flour
    3 teaspoons baking powder
    2 tablespoons sugar
    ½ teaspoon salt
    2 eggs
    ¾ cup sour cream
    1 teaspoon soda dissolved in 2 tablespoons cold water
    1½ cups sweet milk
    1 teaspoon vanilla

1. Sift dry ingredients together.
2. Beat eggs until light; add sour cream, soda dissolved in cold water, sweet milk, vanilla; blend.
3. Add sifted dry ingredients; mix.
4. Heat No. 918 pan over high heat until a small piece of white paper placed in bottom turns brown.
5. Remove paper; reduce heat to medium; pour pancakes.
6. Brown on one side; turn; brown on other side.
7. Yield: 32 cakes, 3 inches in diameter.

BUCKWHEAT CAKES

    About 1 quart lukewarm water
    1 envelope compressed yeast
    2 teaspoons salt
    2 tablespoons sugar or molasses
    2 cups buckwheat flour
    2 cups sifted all purpose flour
    6 tablespoons melted shortening
    ½ teaspoon baking soda

1. Pour 1 cup of the water over yeast; let stand about 10 minutes. Dissolve salt, sweetening in remaining water; add dissolved yeast. Blend liquid mixture with flours. Add shortening; beat until smooth.
2. Let rise until full of bubbles—about one hour. Dissolve soda in 2 tablespoons warm water; stir into batter.
3. Heat No. 918 pan over high heat until a piece of white paper placed in bottom turns brown.
4. Reduce heat to medium-high; pour cakes.
5. Brown on one side; turn; brown on other side.
6. Yield: 24 medium cakes.

FRENCH TOAST

    2 eggs
    2 tablespoons sugar
    ½ teaspoon salt
    1 cup milk
    1 tablespoon melted shortening
    6 slices stale bread

1. Break eggs into bowl; beat well.
2. Add sugar, salt, milk, shortening.
3. Dip bread into mixture; brown on No. 918 pan. When a golden color on one side, turn.
4. Serve either with confectioners' sugar or syrup.